UNDERSTANDING FINANCIAL MATHEMATICS

CONCEPTS AND PRACTICE

CRYFORD MUMBA
(PhD., MBA, B.A, ECon. Adv. Dip. Proj. Mgt, Dip. Banking, Dip. Mkt, ACCA Finalist.)

Order this book online at www.trafford.com
or email orders@trafford.com

Most Trafford titles are also available at major online book retailers.

Printed in the United States of America.

ISBN: 978-1-4269-7391-8 (sc)
ISBN: 978-1-4269-7410-6 (e)

Trafford rev. 06/25/2011

 www.trafford.com

North America & International
toll-free: 1 888 232 4444 (USA & Canada)
phone: 250 383 6864 ♦ fax: 812 355 4082

HOW TO USE THIS BOOK

To benefit from its design you need to know how to use it. The subject is treated under broad topics which form the basis of twelve Chapters.

CHAPTER 1 MATHEMATICAL TECHNIQUES

Provides you with an insight to the world of mathematical techniques. Basic techniques that are useful throughout your subject are introduced.

CHAPTER 2 EXPONENTIAL FUNCTIONS AND INDICES

Encompasses the rules of exponents which are needed for improved calculative abilities.

CHAPTER 3 LOGARITHMIC FUNCTIONS

Adds further to your skills and abilities in numerical analysis. It introduces you to the use of logarithms for many a number of computations.

CHAPTER 4 PROGRESSIONS

Introduces you to some mathematical patterns of adding or multiplying by a constant number. Specifically, the nth term and sum of both arithmetic and geometric progressions are fully covered. The elements of this chapter are also important for computations involved in Chapter 8.

CHAPTER 5 BINOMIAL THEOREM

Introduces you to methodology applied when evaluating and expanding expressions whose the power is greater than 2.

CHAPTER 6 COMPOUNDING AND DISCOUNTING

Concentrates on the key issues relating to the interest computations. It begins with simple interest, simple discount, promissory notes and compounding. This forms the basis for financial mathematics.

CHAPTER 7 INVESTMENT APPRAISAL

Concerns the evaluation of capital investment projects using Net Present Value and Internal Rate of Return techniques. Thus discounting cash flow techniques are fully explored.

CHAPTER 8 ANNUITIES

Building on knowledge gained in chapter 6, this chapter analyses the matters concerning constant payments or receipts of cash over time. Various types of annuities and their computations are fully covered.

CHAPTER 9 BONDS

Concerns the application of Knowledge and skills acquired from earlier Chapters to bonds. An analysis of bond mathematics' is explored in detail.

CHAPTER 10 EXPECTATIONS AND MORTALITIES

Introduces you to annuities applied to endowments, premiums and other related matters. The use of mortality tables is paramount here.

CHAPTER 11 PAST PROGRESS TESTS AND MOCKS

Provides you with a variety of past progress tests and mock exams that were actually written by students at Premier College.

CHAPTER 12 SUGGESTED SOLUTIONS TO PROGRESS CLINICS

Provides you with answers to all the progress clinics covered in the text. Abbreviated and full answers to all questions are given. These should help you check your progress.

CONTENTS   PAGE

Preface.. 14

Dedication 16

Chapter 1   - Introduction.................................... 17

                                 - The Number System 17

Basic Mathematical - Basic Mathematical Operations. 18
Techniques

                                 - Significant Digits 19

                                 - Scientific Notation 20

                                 - Equations....................................... 20

                                 - Percentages, Fractions and
                                    Decimals.. 23

                                 - Discounts 25

                                 - Mark-up and Margin 25

                                 - Ratios 26

                                 - Progress Clinic 1 28

Chapter 2   - Introduction.................................... 33

Exponential   - Laws of exponents 33

Functions and
Indices   - Progress Clinic 2 36

Chapter 3   - Introduction 39

Logarithmic   - Form of Logarithmic Functions 39
Functions

                                 - Properties of Logarithms................... 39

	- Finding the Logarithm of Number..........................	39
	- Antilogarithms	40
	- Using Logarithms	41
	- Common Logarithms........................	41
	- Natural Logarithms	42
	- Progress Clinic 3.............................	45
Chapter 4	- Introduction.....................................	49
Progressions	- Sequences and Series	49
	- Arithmetic progression	49
	- Nth Terms of Arithmetic Progression...................................	50
	- Sum of First nth Terms of Arithmetic Progression	51
	- Geometric Progression	52
	- Nth Term of a Geometric Progression	54
	- Sum of First nth Terms of a Geometric Progression	55
	- Sum of Infinite Geometric Progression	57
	- Progress Clinic 4	58

Chapter 5

Binomial Theorem   - Introduction   61

         - Binomial Theorem   61

         - Progress Clinic 5   70

Chapter 6   - Introduction   71

Compounding   - Simple Interest   71
And Discounting

       - Exact and Ordinary Simple
          Interest   74

       - Exact and Approximate Time.............   76

      - Application Of Simple Interest
         : Promissory Note...........................   80

     - Application of Simple Discount
       : Promissory Note   81

      - Present Value of A Debt   82

      - Equations of Value   84

      - Compounding   87

      - Calculating Compound
         Interest   89

      - Calculating The Compound
         Interest Rate   89

      - Calculating The Number of
         Years...   90

      - Calculating The Amount
         To Be Invested   91

      - Different Types of Investments
         Problems   91

- Compounding and Inflation.............. 92

- Changes In Interest Rate 93

- Increasing The Sum Invested 94

- More Frequent Compounding:
  Nominal And Effective Rates 95

- Compound Amount Under More Frequent
  Compounding................................. 96

- An Addendum 103

- Depreciation 103

- Discounting 107

- Simple Discount 107

- Compound Discount 110

- Progress Clinic 6 112

Chapter 7   - Introduction 115

Capital Investment - Net Present Value 115
Appraisal

- Decision Criteria 116

- Advantages of NPV 117

- Disadvantages of NPV 117

- Internal Rate of Return 117

- Steps to IRR Calculations 118

- Decision Criteria 118

- Advantages of IRR 118

- Disadvantages of IRR 119

- Lease or Buy Decision 121

	- Progress Clinic 7	125
Chapter 8	- Introduction	129
Annuities	- Types of Annuities	129
	- Annuity Factors	130
	- Present Value of An Ordinary Annuity	131
	- Present Value of An Annuity Due.......	132
	- Calculating The Required Annuity......	135
	- Calculating The Required Number of Installments	138
	- Amortization Annuity	139
	- Amortization Schedule	139
	- Sinking Funds	143
	- Sinking Fund Schedule.....................	144
	- Sinking Fund Methods of Depreciation...................................	147
	- Depreciation Schedule	148
	- Perpetuities	150
	- Present Value of Perpetuity	150
	- Progress Clinic 8	151
Chapter 9	- Introduction	153
Bonds	- Key Terms In The Analysis of Bonds....	153
	- Pure Discount or Zero Bond	154

- Present Value of A Pure Discount Bond 154

- Calculating The Yield Rate 155

- Calculating The Required Number of Years 156

- Coupon Bond 157

- Present Value of An Annual Coupon Bond 157

- Present Value of A Semi-Annual Coupon Compound 158

- A Detour in Bond Computations 159

- Calculating The Yield Rate 2 161

- Bond Schedule 163

- Serial Bonds 167

- Treasury Bills Pricing 168

- Progress Clinic 9 170

Chapter 10

Expectations And Mortalities

- Introduction 173

- Expectations 173

- Decision Criteria: Expected Values 173

- Calculating of Expected Value 174

- Expectations and Future Values 176

- Mortality Tables 177

- General Mortality Rules 178

- Alternative Approach to Above Rules 180

- Application of Mortality Tables and Expectation Principles...................... 181

- Cost of A Pure Endowment 182

- An Addendum 183

- Life Annuities 184

- Types of Life Annuity 184

- An Addendum 188

- Life Insurance 189

- Types of Life Insurance Policies 190

- Net Single Premium For Whole Life Insurance.. 190

- Net Single Premium For A Term Insurance.. 191

- Net Single Premium For An Ordinary Term Life 191

- Net Single Premium For An Endowment Insurance.. 192

- Net Single Premium For An Ordinary Endowment Insurance Policy............ 193

- Progress Clinic 10 194

Chapter 11

Past Progress Tests and Mocks   - Variety of Questions Without Suggested Solutions 197

Chapter 12

Solutions to Progress Clinics   - Answers to All Progress Clinic Questions.............................. 209

-    Formula Sheet   246
-    Mortality Tables   252

I hope you will find this compendium useful to significantly contribute to your success in the exams. BON VOYAGE!

ABOUT THE AUTHOR

Dr. Cryford Mumba read Economics at The University of Zambia and graduated with a Bachelor of Arts Degree. He complemented his Economics degree with the Advanced Diploma in Project Management(Institute of Commercial Management, UK), Diploma in Banking and Financial Services(Zambia Institute of Banking and Financial services, Zambia), Diploma in Marketing(ICM, UK). He then expanded his knowledge of business through the accountancy program (ACCA, UK) for which he is a finalist. He holds an MBA(MANCOSA, South Africa) with a thesis "Limited Access to Credit Among Women Market Traders". Finally, he holds a PhD in Economics (Cambell State University, USA) with a thesis "Understanding Money Intelligence".

Dr. Mumba is the Proprietor and Chief Executive Officer of Premier college of Banking and Finance, a firm specializing in financial training and consulting. His specialist teaching areas include Financial Mathematics, Statistical Analysis, Corporate Finance, Financial Reporting and Economics. He has written extensively on banking and financial services course. He is the author of Understanding Money Intelligence, Understanding Statistical Analysis and a host of other Banking and Financial Services training manuals. He is also the Editor of The Student Banker Magazine and a columnist on financial matters for Business analysis Newspaper.
He resides in Lusaka, married and is a supporter of Arsenal Football Club. His hobbies include reading and writing.

PREFACE TO THE SECOND EDITION

If you have bought or are thinking of buying this book you will want to know what you can expect it to do for you and how you ought best to use it.

This is the 2nd edition of the very successful book on financial mathematics. This edition consolidates the success story of the 1st edition with added examples and explanations. The book has been developed from practical teaching of Financial Mathematics. It covers all the numerical analysis required for financial mathematics examination and other courses requiring numerical analysis.

The guiding principles for this book are that it is "user-friendly" with numerous worked examples and related to the current Financial Mathematics Practice. One difficulty encountered in the production of this book is that some students have little or no practical experience of the subject. Therefore, a step-by-step explanation has been adopted which has made me guilty of one offence: "over-simplification". The book can be used with confidence because it is designed to be user-friendly, interesting to read and to stimulate learning by the use of clear examples with detailed solutions. The book seeks to set the subject of Financial Mathematics as enjoyable as any other subject.

At this juncture I should sound some caution. The book provides you with the knowledge and the skills in applying it which you need to pass. However, if you aspire to excel, perhaps even to win a place or a prize, you cannot expect to rely on one book alone! The highest marks are given to those candidates who display evidence of the widest reading absorbed by critical mind, a combination, that is, of extensive information and of a highly intellectual appraisal of it. No single book can provide either of these things. What it can do, however, is to provide an adequate amount of information and acceptable competence in handling it. No doubt Financial Mathematics course will include matters which I have omitted, and some lecturers may not consider all the items I have covered as appropriate. I do hope, however, that a large proportion of the text will be helpful to students of Financial Mathematics.

This text grew out of the Financial Mathematics subject I have been teaching at Premier College of Banking and Finance during the past few semesters. I was very fortunate to have had many excellent students, who with their questions and comments contributed much to the clarity of exposition of this text.

I owe a great intellectual debt to my brilliant former teachers at all levels in my educational radar.

Finally, I would like to express my gratitude to Chileshe Chanda for her efficiency and cheerful disposition in typing the manuscript. This was key to the text's completion.

I shall greatly appreciate the suggestions for further improvement of the book, both from the teachers and students of the subject.

It should be stressed that this book is written to teach you and not merely to tell you. The more work and effort you put into all your studies, the greater the chance of success. Be determined, have a positive attitude and all the very best in your future courses and exams.

Cryford Mumba
29Th June 2011

To my mother Janet Mumba

QUOTATION

"I am a beau in nothing but my books"   **Adam Smith (1723-1790)**.

"A man who kills another man destroys a living creature, but a man who kills a good book kills reason itself" **unknown**.

"If people do not believe that Matheamtics is simple, it is only because they do not realize how complicated life is".   **John Louise Von Neumann (1903 – 1957)**.

CHAPTER 1

BASIC MATHEMATICAL TECHNIQUES

INTRODUCTION

Before one can climb the tree branch, one needs to start from the ground and advance step by step to reach the desired branch to pick the fruits. In the same manner, the study of financial mathematics has got the 'ground' from which one has to start.

This chapter is designed to provide that much needed ground work in this subject. It is important that you review and understand the material covered in this chapter before you can proceed. Specifically, this chapter covers number systems, basic mathematical operations, significant figures, equations, percentages, fractions and decimals, ratios and proportions, and discounts.

THE NUMBER SYSTEM

At some level, 3 − 5 = it can't? This expression is very correct due to limitation of the number available for calculations. The complete number system is made up of the following:

1. **Natural numbers** – these are numbers which start from 1 upwards. Examples are 1, 2, 3, 4, 5, ... Using natural numbers only the answer 3 − 5 = it cant is correct.

2. **Whole numbers** – these are numbers which start from 0 upwards. Examples are 0, 1, 2, 3,................. This is an improvement in the number system though 3 − 5 = it can't remains.

3. **Integers** – these are numbers which range from negative infinite to positive infinite. This represents the number line system. With this system of numbers 3 − 5 is no longer it cant but instead it is -2. Examples of integers are ....-3, -2, -1, 0, 1, 2, 3, ... Thus integers can further be divided into even and odd numbers, prime numbers.

4. **Even numbers** – these are integers divisible by 2 without leaving any remainder. Examples are 2, 4, 6, 8,...............................

5. **Odd numbers** – these are integers which are not even numbers. Examples are 1, 3, 5, 7, ...

6. **Prime Numbers** – these are integers which have only two factors, namely 1 and itself. Examples are 1, 2, 5, 7, 11, 13, 17 ....

7. **Fractions** – these are numbers expressed in the form of a numerator divided by a denominator. Examples are $\frac{3}{5}$, $\frac{1}{3}$, $\frac{4}{13}$, $\frac{-5}{8}$, ...

8. **Decimals** – these are numbers expressed in the form of a number point other numbers. Decimals are divided into **terminating** i.e. those where division terminates or ends at some point, and **repeating** where division

does not terminate or end: it continues with the same digit. Examples of terminating decimals are $\frac{3}{5}$ = 0.6, $\frac{1}{4}$ = 0.25,......................

Examples of repeating decimals are 1/3= 0.33333...........................

which is $0.\bar{3}$ for short, 2/3 = 0.666666 .... Which is $0.\bar{6}$.

9. **Irrational Numbers** – these are numbers like $\sqrt{2}$,$3\sqrt{5}$,....which can be terminating or repeating decimals.

10. **Rational Numbers** – these are integers and common fractions

BASIC MATHEMATICAL OPERATIONS

No matter how complex the combination of digits is for calculation, basic mathematical operations centre around only four elements namely:

- Additional (+)
- Subtraction (-)
- Multiplication (X)
- Division (/)

Sometimes, all the above operations are combined hence the need for the order of operation. The right order of operation is given by the acronym **BODMAS** which can be explained as follows:

- B for Brackets of
- D for Division
- M for Multiplication
- A for Addition
- S for Subtraction

Note that powers and indices are worked out immediately after brackets and before division, multiplication, addition and subtraction.

BASIC RULES

1. (-) x (-) = (+) When two negative numbers are multiplied together, the result is Positive

2. (-) x(+) = (-) When a negative and a positive number are multiplied, the result is negative

3. (+) x (+) = (+) When two positive numbers are multiplied, the result is positive

4. (-) / (-) = (+) When two negative numbers are divided, the result is positive

5. (-) / (+) = (-) When a negative is divided by a positive number, the result is negative

6. (+) / (+) = (+) When two positive numbers are divided, the result is positive

7. (-) + (-) = (-) When two negative numbers are added, the result is negative

8. (-) + (+) = (±) When a negative and a positive number are added, the result is positive or negative

9. (+) + (+) = (+) When two positive numbers are added, the result is positive

10. (-) – (-) = (-) When two negative numbers are subtracted, the result is negative

11. (+) – (+) = (±) When two positive numbers are subtracted, the result is positive or negative

SIGNIFICANT DIGITS

Sometimes a decimal number has too many digits in it for practical use. This problem can be overcome by rounding the decimal number to a specific number of significant figures by discarding digits using the following:

"If the first digit to be discarded is greater than or equal to five, then add one to the previous digit. Otherwise the previous digit is unchanged".

Note that failure to round off digits correctly negatively impacts on your final answer. You will be able to see that most of the calculations involving discount factors, annuity factors, and so on will give you 12 digits from your calculator; (as long as you are using a 12 digit calculator). With such figures when should rounding off be carried out? My simple advice is that you need to use all the figures from the calculator and only round off the final answer to improve accuracy.

Example 1

Round off the following to the specified significant digit:

     (a) 187.392 to five significant figures
     (b) 187.392 to four significant figures
     (c) 187.392 correct to three significant digit

Solution

(a) 187.392 correct to 5 significant digits gives 187.39. Discarding a 2 causes nothing to be added to the 9.

(b) 187.392 correct to 4 significant digits gives 187.4. Discarding the 9 cause's one to be added to the 3.

(c) 187.392 correct to three significant digits gives 187. Discarding a 3 causes nothing to be added to the 7.

SCIENTIFIC NOTATION

A minor (though annoying) disadvantage of the decimal notation is that the decimal point often manages to be misplaced during the course of calculations. For example, 187.392 becomes 187,392, etc. In order to avoid mistakes of this kind, it has become common practice (at least in scientific work) to use what is known as **scientific notation**. In this notation each number is written as a product of a number between 1 and 10 and an appropriate power of 10.

It requires some practice to convert numbers from the ordinary decimal notation to the scientific notation and vice versa, but it is not really difficult. All you have to do is count how many places the decimal point has to be moved to the left or to the right so that we get a number between 1 and 10. If the decimal point has to be moved n places to the left, where n is a positive integer or zero, the exponent of 10 is n: if the decimal point has to be moved n places to the right, the exponent of 10 is –n.

Example 2

Convert the following decimal notations to scientific notations:

a) 346.87
b) 0.000981

Solution

a) For 346.87 the decimal point has to be moved two places to the left (to yield a number between 1 and 10) and we write it as 3.4687×10^2 or simply 3.4687^2

b) For 0.000981 the decimal point has to be moved four places to the right (to yield a number between 1 and 10) and we write it as 9.81×10^{-4} or simply 9.81^{-4} as the calculator would indicate.

Note: 9.81^{-4} does not imply 9.81 raised to the power negative 4, what it means is that you need to move the decimal point 4 places to the left. The same applies to 3.4687^2.

In case you are not familiar with negative exponents, I can point out that $10^{-1} = \frac{1}{10}, 10^{-2} = \frac{1}{100}, 10^{-3} = \frac{1}{1000}$ and in general $10^{-k} = \frac{1}{10^k}$ for any positive integer K : and $10 = 1$ by definition. Further work on exponents may be found in Chapter 4 of this book.

EQUATIONS

Equations provide the exact model for many relationships that arise in business. They are also used to approximate more complicated kinds of relationships, and play a major role in describing the overall pattern of statistical relationships. Paramount to all this is the issue of a formula. Many business and economics applications are described by a specified formula. Examples of formulas you will need to learn in this subject are simple interest, simple discount and compound interest (Chapter 5) ordinary and due annuties(Chapter 8), Progressions (Chapter4), mortalities (Chapter 9) to mention but a few.

In all the above situations, equations with the numbers filled in for all but one of the variables are given. The problem is then to find the number which should be filled in for the last variable. This is called *solving* the equation.

- To solve an equation, we need to get into the form "unknown variable = something with just numbers in it, which we can work out".

- The rule is that you can do what you like to one side of the equation, so long as you do the same thing to the other side straightaway. The two sides are equal, and they will stay equal so long as you treat them in the same way.

For example, you can do any of the following:

- Add 58 to both sides

- Subtract 3x from both sides

- Multiply both sides by 5.2312

- Divide both sides by (x + 5)

- Take the reciprocal of both sides

- Square both sides

- Take the cube root of both sides

Example 3

i) Solve the following equations for x:

a) $10 + x = 16$

b) $3x + 72 = 450$

c) $3x + 2 = 5x = 5x - 7$

d) $\sqrt{\dfrac{3x^2 + x}{2\sqrt{x}}} = 7$

ii) Change the subject of the formula to the one in bracket for each of the following equations.

a) $y = \sqrt{3x + 7}$ (x)

b) $7 + g = \sqrt{\dfrac{5}{h}}$

Solution

a) $10 + x = 16$

$10 - 10 + x = 16 - 10$ i.e. **Subtract** 10 from both sides

$x = 16 - 10$ i.e. work out the right hand side

$x = 6$

Proof: $10 + 6 = 16$

$16 = 16$

b) $3x + 72 = 450$

$3x + 72 - 72 = 450 - 72$ i.e. **subtract** 72 from both sides

$\dfrac{3x + 72 - 72}{3} = \dfrac{}{3}$ i.e. **divide** by 3 both sides

$x = \underline{126}$

c) $3x + 2 = 5x - 7$

$3x + 2 + 7 = 5x - 7 + 7$ i.e **Add** 7 to both sides

$3x + 9 = 5x$

$3x - 3x + 9 = 5x - 3x$ i.e. **subtract** 3x from each side

$9 = 5x - 3x$ i.e. solve right hand side

$\dfrac{9}{2} = \dfrac{2x}{2}$ i.e. divide by 2 both sides

$\underline{4.5 = x}$

d) $\sqrt{\dfrac{3x^2 + x}{2\ \ \ \ \ x}} = 7$

$\dfrac{3x^2 + x}{4x} = 49$ i.e. square each side

$\dfrac{(3x + 1)}{4} = 49$ i.e. cancel x in the numerator and the denominator of the left hand side: this does not affect the value of the hand side, so there is no need to charge the right hand side

$3x + 1 = 196$ i.e. multiply each side by 4

$3x = 195$ i.e. subtract 1 from each side

x = 65 i.e. divide each side by 3

ii) a) $y = \sqrt{3x + 7}$

   $y^2 = 3x + 7$ i.e. square each side

   $y^2 - 7 = 3x$ i.e. subtract 7 from each side

   $x = y^2 - 7$ i.e. divide each side by 3 and swap the two sides for easy
   reading

   b) $7 + g = \dfrac{5}{3\sqrt{h}}$

   $\dfrac{1}{7 + g} = 3\sqrt{\dfrac{h}{5}}$ i.e. take reciprocal of each side.

   $\dfrac{5}{7 + g} = 3\sqrt{h}$ i.e. multiply each side by 5

   $\dfrac{5}{3(7 + g)} = 3\sqrt{h}$ i.e. divide each side by 3

   $h = \dfrac{25}{g(7 + g)^2}$ i.e. square each side, and swap the sides for easy reading.

PERCENTAGES, FRACTIONS AND DECIMALS

A percentage is a number expressed out of 100

Rules

- Turn a fraction or decimal into a percentage we multiply by 100%
- Turn a percentage into a fraction or a decimal we divide by 100

Example: 4 Complete the following table

Fraction	Decimal	Percentage
¼	-	-
-	0.6	-
-	-	50%

Solution

Fraction	Decimal	Percentage
¼	0.25	25%
3/5	0.6	60%
5/10 = ½	0.5	50%

PERCENTAGE INCREASE OR DECREASES

Percentage increase or decrease = New Figure – Original X 100
Original Figure

Example 5

a) The price of a commodity has changed from K10 000 to K15 000. Find the percentage increase in the price of the commodity?

K15 000 – K10 000 X 100
K10 000

K5000 X 100
K10 000

= 50%

b) The price of a certain commodity was initially K10, 000 and has been hiked up by 50%. Find the new price.

50% = x – K10 000 X 100%
             K10 000

1   X 50% = x – K10 000 X 100% X 1/100
100   K10 000

½ = x – K10 000 = ½ X 10 000 = x – 20 000
          K10 000

5000 = x – 10 000 x = ⁻10 000 – 500 = K150000

c) A seller makes a profit of 25% by selling a product at K5000. Find the cost price. (2) find the actual profit made.

Cost price   100%
Profit   + 25%
Selling price   125%
= K5000 X 100
            125

= K4000

Profit = K5000 – K4000

= <u>K1000</u>

e) Find 60% of K4800

= <u>K2880</u>

f) 60% of a number is 2880. Find the number

60% =   2880
100% =   x

x = <u>100 X 2880</u> = 4800
       60

DISCOUNTS

A discount is a reduction on the invoice price. There are generally two types of discount namely:

1) *Cash discount*: this is given to a customer for prompt payment. It is a way a company can try to reduce incidence of bad debts.

2) *Trade discounts*: this is a reduction in the invoice price given by one trader to another for bulk buying. It encourages trade to buy goods from one source.

Example 6

A certain product is priced at K250, 000. There is a 10% discount on the invoice price if the customer pays within 5 days of purchase. If a person buys that product and pays within 3 days find the actual amount he will have to pay?

Solution

Discount = 10% of K250 000 = K25 000.
Amount paid K250 000 – K25 000 = K225 000
The customer will pay only K225 000.

MARK UP AND MARGIN

Profits may be calculated either as a Percentage of sales margin) or as a Percentage cost of sales (mark up).

For mark up we calculate it as:

a) Mark up = <u>Gross Profit</u> X 100%
           Cost Price

b) Margin = <u>Gross Profit</u> X 100%
         Selling Price

a) Mark up in simple terms

Cost of sales (%) + profit (%) = price %

e.g. If cost of sales = 100%
       Plus profit = 25%
       Sales = 125%

Example 7

If the cost price of a product is K10, 000 and retailer has a mark up of 25%. Find the selling price.

Cost Price = 100% being K10, 000 = Cost of Profit = 25%

b) **Margin**

Selling Price 100%
Less Profit 20%
Cost Price 80%

If the selling price of a product is K12500 and the retailer makes a profit (margin) of 20%. Find the cost price.

Mark-up	Margin	
$\frac{1}{4}$	$\frac{1}{4+1} =$	$\frac{1}{5}$
$\frac{2}{11}$	$\frac{2}{11+2} =$	$\frac{2}{13}$

- To turn a mark up into a margin add the nominator or the denominator.

Margin	Mark-up	
$\frac{1}{6}$	$\frac{1}{6-1} =$	$\frac{1}{5}$
$\frac{3}{13}$	$\frac{3}{13-3} =$	$\frac{3}{10}$

- To turn a margin into a mark up. We subtract the numerator from denominator.

RATIOS

A ratio shows the relative size of a component from the whole. To find the relative shares, we first add the ratios. Ratios can be expressed as proportion or percentage or indeed as a fraction.

Example 8

A firm which employs 100 workers has 60%of them makes.

c) Determine the number of females and males employed by the firm.
d) The proportion of male and female

Solution

a) Since a ratio shows the relative size of a component from the whole (total), then the total is 100% so that we have 60% males and 40% females which gives us 60% to 40% respectively

Number of females = 60 X 100 = 60
                          100

b) The proportion of males to females is 3:2

Example 9

a) A, B, C are share K10 000 in the ratio 2 : 3 : 5. How much will each receive?

b) If A, B, and C each receive K2000, K3000 and 5000 respectively by sharing a certain amount of money in the ratio 2 : 3 : 5. Find the total amount being shared?

Solution

a) 2 + 3 + 5 = 10

   A's share is 2 X K10 000 = K2000
                     10

   B's share is 3 X K10 000 = K3000
                     10

C's share is 5 X 10 000 = K5000
                  10

b) 2 + 3 + 5 = 10

   Using A's share 2 x = K2000
                     10

   Where x is the total amount being shared.

 Solving for x, gives x = K2000 X 10 = K10 000
                                    2

Thus, the total amount being shared is K10 000. We can get the same result using either B's or C's share.

PROGRESS CLINIC ONE

1. Convert the following decimals into the scientific notation

    a) 128.9
    b) 0.000138
    c) 12 689.4
    d) 0.0000017
    e) 13 250 499

2. Convert each of the following numbers from the scientific notation to the ordinary decimal notation:

    a) 3.1667×10^3
    b) 1.72^{-2}
    c) 2.577^4
    d) 2.9948×10^{-5}
    e) 6.285×10^7
    f) 8.99931×10^{-6}

3. Convert each of the following fractions into decimals and indicate whether They are terminating or repeating decimals.

    a) $\dfrac{13}{250}$

    b) $\dfrac{9}{11}$

    c) $\dfrac{8}{15}$

    d) $\dfrac{5}{21}$

    e) $\dfrac{7}{20}$

    f) $\dfrac{5}{28}$

    g) $\dfrac{35}{120}$

    h) $\dfrac{121}{625}$

    i) $\dfrac{352}{999}$

4. Express:

    a)   0.625 as a fraction

b) $\underline{125}$ as a percentage
1000

c)   0.375 as a fraction

d) $\underline{3}$ as a decimal
6

e)   3.75 as a percentage

f) $\underline{3}$ as a percentage
4

5. A customer's balance in a savings account increased from K765 200 to K1111450 Cr over a period. What is the percentage increase to 2 decimal places?

6. A customer's balance in a savings account decreased from K1111450 to K765 200 Cr over a period of time. What is the percentage decrease to two decimal places?

7. The price of a job including VAT at 17.5% is K8 430 000. What is the price of the job excluding VAT to the nearest Kwacha.

8. A firm makes 1376 CD Players. The number of walkman, mini and mid- sized models is in the ratio 5 to 16 to 11.

    a) How many walkman CD Players are made?
    b) How many of the mid-sized CD Players are made?

9. a) Suppose Tom and Dick wish to share K20 000 000 out in the ratio 3: 2 respectively. How much will each receive?

    b) A certain amount is to be shared between Tom and Dick from a pick-a-lot draw in the ratio 70% to 30% respectively. If Dick receives K24 000 000, what is the total amount being shared? How much will Tom receive?

10. K700 000 is to be shared out between Mr. Yu, Mr. He and Mr. We in the ratio 8: 5: 1. How much will Mr. Yu receive?

11. Work out the following using your calculator.

    f) $(18.6)^{2.6}$

    g) $(18.6)^{-2.6}$

    h) $2.6\sqrt{18.6}$

    i) $(14.2)^{4} \times (14.2)^{\frac{1}{4}}$

j) $(14.2)^4 + (14.2)^{1/4}$

k) $(70 + 2)^{/12} + (33 - 6)^{/-3}$

12. A salesman's weekly wage is made up of a basic weekly wage of K100 000 and commission of K5000 for every item he sells. Derive an equation which describes this scenario. Using the equation derived, determine how much the salesman would receive in a week if he sells 20 items.

13. Solve for x for each of the following:

a) $4\sqrt{x} + 32 = 40.618$

b) $x^3 = 4.913$

c) $34x - 7.6 = (17x - 3.8) \times (x + 12.5)$

d) $\frac{2}{3}x = \frac{1}{2}$

e) $2x + 7 = x + 9$

f) $-11x = -55$

14. Change the subject of the formula to the one in brackets for each of the following:

a) $A = 0.5bh$ (h)

b) $A = \pi r^2$ (r)

(c) $P = 2w + 21$ (l)

15. a) Consider the formula

$$K = \frac{J}{R - 2(M + R)}$$

i) If K = 8, R = 1 and M = ½, what is the value of J?

ii) Using the same value of K, what is $K^2 + \sqrt{\dfrac{K}{2}}$

b) Simplify $\dfrac{1}{1.1} S^2 \div (1 - \dfrac{1}{1.1})$

c) In the equation C = 6000 + 0.5Q C denotes the total cost of sales (in thousands of kwacha) and Q denotes the number of units sold (in thousands). What is the total cost of sales for 3000 units to 2 decimal places.

16. A firm which sells special articles provides 20% discount on each item for prompt payment and 10% discount for bank purchase. Mr. Price buys articles for K25 000 000:

   a) Calculate the cash discount for Mr. Price if he pays promptly

   b) Calculate the trade discount for Mr. Price if the purchase of articles worth K25 000 000 is considered bulk purchase by the seller.

   c) If Mr. Price qualifies for both cash and trade discount how much will he actually pay for the articles?

17. A business college offering training in Banking and Finance charges K700 000 per subject at certificate level. The colleges gives a discount of K50 000 for any additional subject taken by a student.

   a) If a student takes 4 subjects, determine how much the student should pay.

   b) Another college charges a flat fee of K400 000 per subject regardless of the number of subjects taken at certificate level. Which college charges the highest tuition fees for 4 certificate level subjects? Holding all other factors constant, where would you recommend the student to do his studies?

CHAPTER 2

EXPONENTIAL FUNCTIONS AND INDICES

INTRODUCTION

In this chapter, we shall study exponential functions. Exponential functions provide important models for the description of economic growth and for most any kind of growth. A very simple example of an exponential function arises in the study of compound interest. Our main thrust in this chapter is to demonstrate the laws of exponents, with which most of you are probably familiar from secondary algebra.

Laws of Exponents

The exponential notation is a mathematical kind of shorthand which dates back to the early part of the 17th century. It saves space and time, and it makes it easy or at least easier, to write otherwise unwieldy expressions.

Generally, if n is a positive integer, we write

$$b^n = \underbrace{b \times b \times b \times ....b}_{\text{n factors}}$$

For any real number b

Here n is called the exponent of b and we read b as "the nth power of b" or as "b raised to the power n". The exponential notation immediately found wider acceptance among mathematicians who soon discovered that there are certain rules about the manipulation of exponents which provide extraordinary simplifications. There are rules for *adding exponents*, *multiplying exponents*, *dividing exponents*, and *subtracting exponents*. The following are the laws of exponents.

Given $2^4 = 16$ i.e. $2x2x2x2 = 16$

2 = base
4 = index or power
2 = raised to the power 4 = 16

Rule 1. *When two numbers with a similar base are being multiplied we add the Powers.*

Example 1

$$x^a \times x^b = x^{a+b}$$

$$2^3 \times 2^2 = 2^5 = 32$$

Rule 2. *When two numbers with the similar base are being divided we simply subtract the powers*

Example 2

$$x^a \div x^b = x^{a-b}$$

$$2^5 \div 2^3 = 2^2 = 4$$

NOTE: $2^5 + 2^3$ is not equal to 2^{5+3}

It should be noted from above that the adding or subtraction of the powers can only be done when multiplication and division are involved.

Rule 3. *Any number raised to the power 1 is the number itself.*

Example 3

$$x^1 = x$$

$$316^1 = 316$$

Rule 4. *Any number raised to the power 0 is equal to 1.*

Example 4

$$x^0 = 1$$

$$316^0 = 1$$

Rule 5. *Negative power: Any number raised to a negative number will give a reciprocal of that number.*

Example 5 $\qquad x^{-1} = \dfrac{1}{x}$

$$\text{e.g. } 2^{-1} = \dfrac{1}{2}$$

Rule 6. *Multiplication of powers*

Example 6

$$(x^{ab}) = x^{a \times b} = x^{ab}$$

$$(2^{2 \times 3}) = 2^6 = 64$$

Rule 7. Positive *fractional powers*

Example 7

$$X^{n/m} = (\ ^m\sqrt{x}\ )^n$$

$$16^{1/2} = (\sqrt{16}\ )^1 = 4^1 = 4$$

$$16^{3/4} = (\ ^4\sqrt{16}\ )^3 = 2^3 = 8$$

Rule 8. *Negative fractional powers*

Example 8

$$X^{-n/m}$$

$$= (\ ^m\sqrt{\dfrac{1}{X}}\ )^n$$

$$= \ ^m\sqrt{\dfrac{1}{x}}\ )^n$$

$$= 16^{-3/4}$$

$$= (\ ^4\sqrt{\dfrac{1}{16}}\ )^3$$

$$= \tfrac{1}{8}$$

Rule 9. *Division using single power*

$$(y/x)^n = \dfrac{y^n}{X^n}$$

$$= \frac{y^n}{x_n}$$

Example 9

$$= (\tfrac{1}{3})^2$$

$$\frac{1^2}{3^2}$$

$$= \frac{1}{9}$$

PROGRESS CLINIC 2

1. Using the laws of exponents, simply each of the following:

    a) $\dfrac{8 \times 256}{32 \times 4}$

    b) $\dfrac{(7^2)^3 (7^{-5})^2}{7^3 (7^4)^{-2} 7^0}$

    c) $81^{3/4}$

    d) $125^{1/3}$

    e) $125^{-1/3}$

    f) $32^{-3/5}$

2. Simplify each of the following

    a) $\dfrac{x^4 \times x^{-5}}{x^2 \times x^3}$

    b) $\dfrac{x^2 y^3}{(3xy)^4}$

    c) $\dfrac{(x/y)^2 y^3}{x}$

3. Evaluate each of the following quantities

    a) $\sqrt[3]{\dfrac{125}{8}}$

b) $\left(\dfrac{1}{5}\right)^{-3}$

c) $625^{-3/4}$

d) $64^{5/6}$

4. If n is a positive odd integer and b is a positive real number, it is customary to refer to $(-b)^{1/n}$ as a real nth root of $-b$ and write it

$\sqrt[n]{-b}$. For instance, $\sqrt[3]{-27} = -3$ since $\sqrt[3]{27} = 3$ and it should be noted that $(-3)^3 = -27$. Use this definition to evaluate the following quantities

a) $\sqrt[3]{-125}$

b) $(-32)^{\frac{1}{5}}$

c) $\sqrt[5]{-243x^{15}}$

d) $\left(\dfrac{-27}{64}\right)^{1/3}$

CHAPTER 3

LOGARITHMIC FUNCTIONS

INTRODUCTION

The logarithm of a number is the power of that number. Logarithmic functions are usually studied because of the role which they play in numerical computations. Logarithmic functions are inverse of the exponential functions discussed in Chapter 2.

FORM OF LOGARITHMIC FUNCTIONS

Given $y = b^x$ is an exponential function with b as the base and x as the power. To convert this exponential function into a logarithmic function, all we need to do is to solve for x as follows:

$X = \log_b y$ which reads" x is the logarithm of y to the base b." Thus log b y is the power to which we have to raise b to get y.

It is important to remember that any question concerning a logarithmic function, its values or its graph, can always be answered by referring to the corresponding exponential functions and vie versa. For instance, y $\log_2 x = x = 2^y$ and $x = \log_2 4 = 4 = 2^x$ in exponential form which follows that x = 2 hence $\log_2 4 = 2$.

The logarithm of a number is the power of that number

Thus, $2^4 = 16$ is equivalent to $\log 2^{16} = 4$

$2^4 = 16$ is in exponential form

Log $2^{16} = 4$ is in log form

PROPERTIES OF LOGARITHMS

1. $\log a^{(xy)} = \log a^x + \log^y a$ (when there is multiplication add the power)

2. Log (x/y) = $\log a^x - \log a^y$
    p

3. Log $a^x = p \log a^x$

4. Log $a^1 = \log a^a = 1$

FINDING THE LOGARITHM OF ANY NUMBER

A log of any number consist of the parts a decimal fraction called **Mantissa** and a whole number called **Characteristic**.

The **Mantissa** is obtained from log tables or calculator. The characteristic is obtained from the following rule, in the number whose log is required move the decimal point until it comes immediately after the first no zero digit. The characteristic is equal to the number of places by which the decimal point is moved. If moved to the left characteristic is positive and if moved to the right it is negative.

NOTE: That table can be used to find logs for any number which is positive. The log of any number between 1 and 10 lies in the range 0 to 1

```
0           .2513————  Mantissa
 |
 |
 |_____  Characteristic
```

Example 1. Find log of 0.2513

Solution

$$= 2.513 \quad = 0.4002 \text{ mantissa}$$

$$\text{characteristic} = {}^{-}1$$

$$\text{Log} = 0.2513$$

$$= {}^{-}1 + 0.4002$$

$$= {}^{-}1 .4002$$

Example 2. Find the log 211.6

Solution

$$\text{characteristic} = 2$$

$$\text{Mantissa } 2.116 = 0.3255$$

$$\text{Log } 2.116 = 2 + 0.3255$$

$$= 2.3255$$

Example 3. Find the Log of 2.15

Solution

$$\text{Characteristic} = 0$$

$$\text{Mantissa} \quad = 0.3324$$

ANTILOGARITHMS

The purpose is simply to convert back from the log number it presents. If tables are used, this can be done by using tables backwards.

Example 4

Find antilog of (a) 0.3564 = 2.2719

b) 2.6444 = 440.96 = 441

Procedure

1. Press shift
2. Log
3. The number 0.3564

USING LOGARITHMS

From the law of indices if two numbers are to be multiplied, their logs are to be added and if one number is to be divided by another, the log of the second number must be subtracted from the log of the first. The answer to the original calculation is found by taking the antilog of the result.

Example 5

Evaluate 5.436 X 0.31

Set is as follows

Number	Log
5.436	0.7353
0.31	$\bar{1}$.4914 add
1.686	0.2267 antilog = 1.686

Evaluate 0.07486 X 0.985 ÷ 62.38

Number	Log		Notes:
0.07486	$\bar{2}$.8742		$\bar{2} + \bar{1} = \bar{3}$
0.985	$\bar{1}$.9934	Add	$\bar{2} - \bar{1} = \bar{3}$
0.073737	$\bar{2}$.8676		$^{-}2 - 1 = ^{-}3$
62.38	1.7950 Subtract		$\bar{3} + \bar{1} = \bar{2}$
0.001182	$\bar{3}$.0726		

COMMON LOGARITHMS

Logarithms to the base 10 are called **common logarithms** or **Briggsian** logarithms, named after the English Mathematician Henry Briggs, who published the first table of logarithms to the base 10 early in the 17th century. Since logarithms to base 10 are widely used in simplifying calculations, it has become common practice to drop the subscript and write $\log_{10}N$ simply as log N.

Note that $\log_{10} 10 = k.\log_{10} 10^{k} = k$ since $\log_{10} 10 = 1$. This follows directly from the definition of the logarithm of a number as the power to which the base has been raised so that it will equal the given number.

NATURAL LOGARITHMS

Natural logarithms which are also called Napierian logarithms (named after the 16th century Scottish Mathematician John Napier, are simply logarithms to the base e = 2.71828...................

So far we have discussed only logarithms to the base 10. They are by far the most widely used in practical computations, but as we have indicated earlier. There are certain theoretical advantages to working with natural logarithms.

It is customary to abbreviate $\log_e N$ to $|n\,N$, which reads "the natural logarithm of N". The natural logarithm of any number can be determined directly using a scientific calculator by pressing the $|n$ button. Alternatively, we can obtain the natural logarithm of any number by making use of the formula:

In N = $\dfrac{\log N}{\log e}$ = $\dfrac{\log N}{0.4343}$ (approximately).

COMPUTATIONS WITH NATURAL LOGARITHMS

We shall not study natural logarithms in much detail but since exponential functions are often given with the base **e**, let us indicate briefly how to change $y = a.b^x$ so that the base of the exponential function becomes e. All we really have to do is change to b^x so that it equals **e** raised to some power, say, e^z. Thus $bx = e^z$, and if we make use of the fact that the logarithm of two equal numbers are equal, we can write:

$|n\,bx = |n\,e^z$ and hence, $x\,(|n\,b) = z\,(|n\,e) = z$ Since In e = $\log_e e = 1$. Thus $bx = e^{x\,(In\,b)}$ and we can write $y = a.e^{x\,(In\,b)}$ instead of $y = a.b^x$ where $|n\,b$ will have to be obtained from the calculator directly or with the use of the formula $|n\,N = \dfrac{\log N}{0.4343}$.

Example 6

The relationship between the price and demand for a new product is given by the equation $D = 1289\,(0.93)^p$ change the above equation to incorporate e.

Solution

D = $1280_e{}^{p}\,(|n\,0.93)$

$|n\,0.93$ gives -0.072570692 directly from calculator.

Alternatively, $\ln 0.93 = \dfrac{\log 0.93}{0.4343} = \dfrac{-0.31517051}{0.4343} = -0.072569769$

This is -0.0726 to 4 decimal places.

Thus, the equation can be written as:

$D = 1280e^{-0.0726p}$

Example 7

How long will it take a sum of money to double it earns 4.5% annual interest, compounded quarterly (use logarithms).

Solution

Let p be the initial investment and 2p be the terminal amount.

$2p = p \left(1 + \dfrac{0.045}{4}\right)^{4t}$

$2p = p (1 + 0.01125)^{4t}$

$\dfrac{2p}{P} = \dfrac{p (1.01125)^{4t}}{p}$

$2 = (1.01125)^{4t}$

Taking logarithms on both sides.

$\ln (2) = 4t \ln (1.01125)$

$4t = \dfrac{\ln (2)}{\ln (1.01125)} = \dfrac{0.69314718}{0.011187189}$

$4t = 61.95901222$

$t = 15.48975306$

$= 15$ years.

Note: Check the answer by using the rules of indices what could have been the result had we used common logarithms instead of natural logarithms? The answer is the same, is it? Prove it!

Example 8

Solve for x: $(1 + x)^{12} = 1.8842$ using logarithms.

Solution

$(1 + x)^{12} = 1.8842$

$12 \ln (1 + x) = \ln (1.8842)$

$\ln (1 + x) = \dfrac{\ln (1.8842)}{12} = 0.052791943$

Taking exponential on both sides:

$1 + x = e^{\,0.052791943}$

$1 + x = 1.054210286$

$x = 0.054210286$

$= 0.0542$

Note: Again we could get the answer using rules of indices quickly. Further $e^{\,0.052791943} = 1.054210286$, to get that figure, we shift and then press the $\ln$ button, enter 0.052791943 and equal button finally.

Example 9

Evaluate

$$\dfrac{0.65 \times 0.0025}{\sqrt[3]{0.001125}} \qquad \text{correct to 4 decimal places using logarithms.}$$

Solution

$$\dfrac{60.65 \times 0.0025}{\sqrt[3]{0.001125}} = \dfrac{60.65 \times 0.0025}{(0.001125)^{1/3}}$$

Using the rules of logarithms, we have:

$\ln (60.65) + \ln (0.0025) - 1/3 \; \ln (0.001125)$

$4.105119635 - 5.991464547 + 1/3 \, (6.78992243)$

$= 4.105119635 - 5.991464547 + 2.263324081 = 0.376979169$

= 0.36979169

= 0.3770

Note: Work out the same question using common logarithms and compare the results.

PROGRESS CLINIC 3

1. Change each of the following equations from the exponential form to the logarithm form.

   a) $9 = 7^x$

   b) $15 = b^4$

   c) $Y = 12^{\frac{1}{2}}$

   d) $Y = 15^{\frac{1}{3}}$

   e) $112 = 3^x$

   f) $200 = b^7$

2. Change each of the following logarithms by putting it equal to x and changing, the equation thus obtained into the exponential form.

   a) $\log_2 64$

   b) $\log_{\frac{1}{3}} 9$

   c) $\log_7 49$

   d) $\log_{11} 11$

3. Verify $\log_b b = 1$ and $\log_b 1 = 0$ for any positive number b by changing each of these equations into the exponential form.

4. Solve for n given that:

   a) $P(1.1)^n = 2P$

   b) $1 - (1.07)^{-n} = 0.491650705$

5. Find the mantissa and characteristic, including the common logarithm of each of the following:

   a) 23.6

   b) 635

   c) 0.00236

d) 0.0000 00001

e) 8 700 000 000

f) 2.09

6. Find the number, the antilogarithm, which corresponds to each of the

a) 1.3729

b)

c) 2.8028

d) -9

e) 9.9395

f) 0.3201

7. Using logarithms, evaluate the following expressions

a) $\dfrac{(285)\,(0.124)}{16.3}$

b) $\sqrt[3]{17.3}$

c) $(0.146)\,(3.72)\,(16.5)$

8.   It is expected that in Lusaka City, the number of families with incomes in x kwacha or more in 2020 will be given by $= 6000\,000x^{-0.8}$. (Note: The equation used in this example, or better its graph is usually referred to as a Pareto curve, named after the Italian economist viltredo Pareto who first suggested the use of curves of this kind in connection with the distribution of incomes).

(a) How many families in Lusaka Should have incomes of K5000 or more in 2020?

(b) How many families in Lusaka should have incomes of K12000 or more in 2020?

(c) How many families in Lusaka should have incomes of K100 000 or more in 2020?

9. In an inventory problem, the total cost of maintaining inventory is a minimum when the size of each order (in packages) is given by

$$x = \sqrt{\dfrac{2KR}{1}}$$

Where K is the cost of placing an order (in kwacha).
R is the monthly demand in packages

I is the cost (in kwacha) of carrying a package in inventory for a month.

What is this optimum order size when K = K7.00, R = 5000 packages, and I = K0.25?

10. (a) How long will it take a sum of money to quadruple, if it earns 7.5% annual interest, compounded monthly?

(b) Solve for n: $(1.05)^n = 4$, using logarithms.

(c) Evaluate $\dfrac{70.75 \times 0.0284}{\sqrt[3]{0.0050246}}$, using logarithms.

11. At what annual interest, compounded quarterly will a sum of money invested now treble after about 15 years?

CHAPTER 4

PROGRESSIONS

INTRODUCTION

In grade 7 examination, there is a paper called special paper 1 which we all have undertaken at that level. Among other types of questions in this paper is that where the candidate is asked to calculate", predict: or "guess" the next two, three, four, and so on digits from given sequence. The same applies to people taking aptitude tests.

To find the next digits in either case, for sequence we must know the rule or pattern by which the sequence is defined. So there should not be guesswork: we need to calculate the digits.

Progressions have a very special role to play in Financial Mathematics and many business applications. In this chapter, we will discuss the two main types of progressions, how to calculate the nth term of each type, how to calculate the sum of the first n terms of each and the derivation of relevant formula.

SEQUENCE AND SERIES

A sequence is a succession of numbers, of which each number is formed according to a definite law which is the same throughout the sequence. When each term in the sequence is summed the result is called a **series**.

There are two types of progression namely Arithmetic Progression and Geometric Progression. For each type we need to know how to calculate the nth term and the sum of the first n terms of a progression.

ARITHMETIC PROGRESSION

An arithmetic progression (AP) is one in which each term is formed from the preceding one by **Adding** a constant number. This constant number which must be added is called the **common difference** (d).

- To find the common difference, all we need is to come up with a simple equation using any of the two numbers which are next to each other.

Example 1

Find the common difference of the following arithmetic progressions:

   a) 2, 3, 4, 5,..

   b) ‑7, 3, 13, 23,...

   c) 22, 20.5, 19,...

Solution

a) The common difference for this one seems obvious. But for some sequences it may not be so hence the need for a simple equation. Thus, we need a number d which when added to or subtracted from 2 we shall get 3, or when added to or subtracted from 4 we get 5 and so on.

- Using the first two digits,

  2 + d = 3, hence d = 3 - 2 = 1

- Using 4 and 5

  4 + d = 5, hence d = 5 – 4 = 1

Thus, whichever digits we can pick as long as they are next to each other, we will get 1 as the constant number being added in this case. The common difference is therefore 1.

b) For ⁻7, 3, 13, 23, ...

- Using ⁻7 and 3,

  ⁻7 + d = 3, hence d = 3 + 7 = 10

The common difference is 10 and can be proved by using any other sets like 13 and 23, etc.

c) For 22, 20.5, 19,.......................................

- Using 20.5 and 19

  20.5 + d = 19, hence d = 19 – 20.5 = ⁻1.5

The common difference here is ⁻1.5 which is subtracted from the preceding one. Thus 22 – ⁻1.5 = 20.5, 20.5 – ⁻1.5 = 19, and so on.

NOTE: *that for any calculation involving the arithmetic progression will require you to know the common difference first.*

Nᵀᴴ TERM OF AN ARITHMETIC PROGRESSION

The nth term of an arithmetic progression is calculated using the formula below:

$$n^{th} \text{ term} = a + (n - 1)d$$

Where a = first term in the sequence
d = common difference
n = the required number of terms

The formula for the nth term of an arithmetic progression is easy to derive:

Writing the first term as a, a + d, a + 2d, a + 3d, a + 4d, a + 5d, ... It can be seen that the coefficient of d is always _one less_ than the number of the term, so that in general:

nth term = a + (n − 1)d as given above.

Example 2

Find the 10th term of the following arithmetic progressions:

(d)   22, 20.5, 19, ...
(e)   -7, 3, 13, ...

Solution

a) From example 1, the common difference has already been calculated to be -1.5

Using nth term = a + (n − 1)d   Where n = 10
                                                                         a = -7
                                                                         d = +10

We have 10th term = -7 + (10 − 1) 10
                               = -7 + (9) (10)
                               = -7 + 90
                               = 83

NOTE: _BODMAS has to be followed in all these calculations to get correct   results._

SUM OF THE FIRST N TERMS OF AN ARITHMETIC PROGRESSION

The sum of the first nth terms of an arithmetic progression is calculated by the following formula:

$$S_n = \frac{n}{2} (2a + (n - 1)d)$$

Where a = first term of the progression
          d = common difference
          n = number of the required terms

The above formula can be derived letting denote l the nth term. The sum of the first n terms of an arithmetic progression with the first term a and the common difference d as:

$S_n = a + (a + d) + (a + 2d) + \ldots\ldots\ldots + (l - 2d) + (l - d) + l.$

Note that the common difference d is subtracted rather than added, when we go backward starting with the nth term. In fact, if we completely invert the order of the terms, we can write the sum of the first n terms as:

$S_n = 1 + (1 + d) + (1 + 2d) + \ldots\ldots\ldots\ldots(a + 2d) + (a + d) + a$ and if we add these two progressions for S_n, we get:

$2S_n = a + (a + d) + (a + 2d) + \ldots\ldots + (1- 2d) + (1 - d) + 1 + 1 + (1 - d) + (1 - 2d)$

$+\ldots\ldots\ldots(a + 2d) + (a + d) + a.$

Now if we pair wise add the terms which we have written one beneath the other, the d's will cancel out and we will always get a + 1, so that:

$2S_n = (a + 1) + (a + 1) + \ldots\ldots\ldots (a + 1) +(a + 1) = n (a + 1)$

And finally, we get $S_n = \dfrac{n (a + 1)}{2}$

Making use of the fact that l is the nth term of an arithmetic progression, we have the following:

$S_n = \dfrac{n}{2} (2a + (n - 1)d)$

Example 3

Find the sum of the first 10 terms of the following arithmetic progressions:

a) 22, 20.5, 19, ...

b) 7, 3, 13,...........................

Solution

a) For 22, 20.5, 19,............   n = 10, d = -1.5, a = 22

using $S_n = \dfrac{n}{2} \left[2a + (n - 1) \right] d$

$S_{10} = \dfrac{10}{2} \left[\; 2 (22) + (10 - 1) \; ^-1.5 \; \right]$

$= 5(44 + (^-13.5)$

$= 5 (30.5)$

$= \underline{152.5}$

GEOMETRIC PROGRESSION (GP)

A geometric progression (GP) is a series in which each term is found by **multiplying** the previous term by a constant number.In a geometric progression, digits may be presented as fractions, fractional powers or decimals connected by either a plus, minus or a comma.

The constant number which is multiplied is called the **common ratio** (R)

To find the common ratio (R), we need to come of the two numbers in the series which are next to each other, just like when finding the common difference (d) for an arithmetic progression.

Example 4

Find the common ratio (R) for each of the following geometric progressions.

a) $\frac{1}{3}$, $\frac{1}{9}$, $\frac{1}{27}$, $\frac{1}{81}$, ...

b) 1, 2, 4, 8, 16 ....

c) 5, 7.5, 11.25, ...

Solution

a) For $\frac{1}{3}$, $\frac{1}{9}$, $\frac{1}{27}$, $\frac{1}{81}$, ...

Above could be presented as $1/3 + 1/9 + 1/27 + 1/81 + ...$ Or as $1/3 + 1/3^2 + ...$

- We can pick the first and second term and connecting them, the first term being multiplied by the constant number R to get the second term.

  Thus, $\frac{1}{3} R = \frac{1}{9}$

  Solving for $R = \frac{1}{9} \times \frac{3}{1} = \frac{1}{3}$ hence $R = \frac{1}{3}$

- We can even pick the third and fourth terms as follows:

  $\frac{1}{27} R = \frac{1}{81}$

  $R = \frac{1}{81} \times \frac{27}{1} = \frac{1}{3}$

b) For 1, 2, 4, 8, 16, ...

   We can pick the third and fourth terms:

   $4R = 8$, $R = \frac{8}{4} = 2$, hence $\underline{r = 2}$

c) For 5, 7.5, 11.25 ....

   We can pick the second and third terms:

   $7.5 R = 11.25$

$$R = \frac{11.25}{7.5} = 1.5, \text{ hence } \underline{R = 1.5}$$

NOTE *that the common ratio (R) is needed for any geometric progression calculation you may wish to undertake hence the need to know how to determine it out-rightly.*

Nᵀᴴ TERM OF A GEOMETRIC PROGRESSION

The nth term of a geometric progression is calculated using the formula below:

$$n^{th} \text{ term} = AR^{n-1}$$

Where A = first term of a geometric progression
   R = common ratio of a geometric progression
   n = required term

NOTE*: that when using the above formula, it is only the common ratio (R) which is raised to the power n-1. This must be worked out first and the answer multiplied by the first term A in that order. The common mistake that you should avoid is to first multiply A by R and then raise the answer to the power n-1.*

The formula for the nth term of a geometric progression is easy to derive. Writing the first few terms as $A, AR, AR^2, AR^3, AR^4, AR^5, \ldots$it can be seen that the exponent of R is always *one less* than the number of the corresponding term, so that in general n^{th} term = AR^{n-1} for any positive integer n.

Example 5

If the first term of a geometric progression is A = 128 and the common ratio R = -½ , find the 5th, 11th and 14th terms respectively.

Solution

n^{th} term = AR^{n-1}

For n = 5, A = 128, R = -½

5th term = $128(-½)^{5-1} = 128(-½)^4 = 128 \times 0.0625 = \underline{8}$

For n = 11, A = 128, R = -½

11th term = $128(-½)^{11-1} = 128(-½)^{10} = 128 \times 0.0009765662 = 0.125$ or ⅛

For n = 14, A = 128, R = -½

14th term = $128(-½)^{14-1} = 128(-½)^{13} = 128 \times {}^-0.00012207 = {}^-0.015628$ or ⁻1/64.

SUM OF THE FIRST N TERMS OF A GEOMETRIC PROGRESSION

The sum of the first n terms of a geometric progression is calculated using the following formula:

$$S_n = \frac{A(1 - R^n)}{1 - R} \text{ for } R < 1$$

or

$$S_n = \frac{A(R^n - 1)}{R - 1} \text{ for } R > 1$$

Where n = required terms
R = common ratio
A = first term

The first of the above two with the first term A and a common ratio R, with n terms has a sum which can be determined as follows:

$S_n = A + AR + AR^2 + AR^3 + \ldots\ldots + AR^{n-2} + AR^{n-1}$ if we multiply the expressions on both sides of the equation by R, we get:

$RS_n = R(A + AR^2 + AR^3 + \ldots\ldots AR^{n-2} + AR^{n-1}) = AR + AR^2 + AR^3 + AR^4 + \ldots\ldots +$

$AR^{n-1} + AR^n$ and if we then subtract "equals" namely the expressions on both sides of the equation RS_n from those of the equation S_n, we get:

$$S_n - RS_n = (A + AR + AR^2 + AR^3 + \ldots\ldots AR^{n-2} + AR^{n-1})$$

$$-(AR + AR^2 + AR^3 + AR^4 + \ldots\ldots + AR^{n-1} + AR^n)$$

Since each term except A and AR^n is added as well as subtracted on the right-hand side of this last equation, we are left with:

$$S_n - SR_n = A - AR^n$$

Which can also be written as?
$$S_n (1 - R) = A (1 - R^n)$$

Finally, dividing by (1 – R) we get

$$S_n = \frac{A(1 - R^n)}{1 - R}$$

Which is the desired formula for the sum of the first n terms of a geometric progression provided that R does not equal 1? (If R equal 1, the terms of the progressions are all equal to A, and above formula cannot be used). However, it is difficult to find non-trivial applications of the above formula in problems of business or economics.

Example 6

Calculate the sum of the first 6 terms of the following series.

a) 5, 7.5, 11.25, ...

b) $\frac{1}{3}, \frac{1}{9}, \frac{1}{27}, \frac{1}{81}$,.............................

Solution

The common ratios (R) for each of the above have already been determined in example 4:

$S_n = \dfrac{A\,(R^n-1)}{R-1}$

a) n = 6
R = 1.5
A = 5

$S_6 = \dfrac{5(1.5^6 - 1)}{1.5 - 1} = \dfrac{5(1.5^6 - 1)}{0.5}$

$= \dfrac{5(1.5^6 -1)}{0.5} = \dfrac{5(11.390625) - 1}{0.5} = \dfrac{5(10.390625)}{0.5}$

$= \dfrac{51.953125}{0.5} = 103.90625 = \underline{103.91}$

b) n = 6
$R = \frac{1}{3}$
$A = \frac{1}{3}$

$S_6 = \dfrac{\frac{1}{3}\left(\frac{1}{3}^6 -1\right)}{\frac{-2}{3}}$

$= \dfrac{\frac{1}{3}\left(\frac{1}{729} - 1\right)}{\frac{-2}{3}}$

$= \dfrac{\frac{1}{3}\left(\frac{-728}{729}\right)}{\frac{-2}{3}}$

=$\frac{728}{2187}$ X $\frac{-3}{2}$

= $\frac{2184}{4374}$

Alternatively, we can use our calculator by changing fractions into decimals as follows:

$\frac{0.333333333 \ (0.333333333^6 - 1)}{0.\ 333333333 - 1}$

= $\frac{0.\ 333333333 \ (0.998628257)}{-\ 0.666666667}$

= $\underline{0.4993128}$

SUM OF INFINITE GEOMETRIC PROGRESSION

The sum an infinite (∞) geometric progression i.e. the progression which continues forever is given by the following formula.

$$S \infty = \frac{A}{1 - R}$$

Where A = first term of a geometric progression
    R = common ratio
    ∞ = infinite number

NOTE *that the above formula is exactly derived in the same manner as any other sum of a geometric progression.*

$S \infty = \frac{A \ (1 - R \infty)}{1 - R}$

But if -1 < R < + 1, as n gets larger R^n gets smaller, hence R^∞ becomes 0.

So $S \infty = \frac{A \ (1 - 0)}{1 - R}$

$\qquad = \frac{A}{1 - R}$

Hence the formula required for infinite sum of a geometric progression.

Example 7

Find the sum of the following geometric progressions which continues forever:

a) 5, 7.5, 11.25, ...

b) $\frac{1}{3}$, $\frac{1}{9}$, $\frac{1}{27}$, $\frac{1}{81}$, ...

Solution

$$S\infty = \frac{A}{1-R}$$

a) $A = 5$

$R = 1.5$

$$S\infty = \frac{5}{1-1.5}$$

$$= \frac{5}{-0.5}$$

$$= -10$$

b) $S\infty = \dfrac{\frac{1}{3}}{1-\frac{1}{3}}$

$$= \dfrac{\frac{1}{3}}{-\frac{2}{3}}$$

$$= \frac{1}{3} \times \frac{-3}{2}$$

$$= \frac{-3}{6} = -\frac{1}{2}$$

FINAL REMARKS ON PROGRESSIONS

This chapter covered all the tenets of progressions. Progressions may be presented as fractions, decimals, whole numbers, integers, and so on. It is advisable that when the series is in form of fractions, the answer must be a fraction as well; If the series is presented as decimals, the answer must be a decimal. This will facilitate cross-checking of your answers. For example, if the figures were increasing by adding a common difference, the sum should surely be greater than any of the terms given in the series.

Progressions, especially the sum of a geometric progression formula is the cornerstone to work on annuities (chapter 8). Make sure you understand this chapter before proceeding.

PROGRESS CLINIC 4

1. a) Calculate the 10th term and the sum of the first 10 numbers of the

   following series: 5, 7.5, 11.25,...................

   b) Calculate the 6th term and the sum of the first 6 terms of the series

   5, 2.5, 1.25, ...

2. a) Find the 21st term of the following series 3, 5, 7, ...

    b) A new company makes 250 products in the first week. If the rate at which these are produced increases by 6 each week, find:

        i)   How many will be produced in their 40th week of manufacture.
        ii)   The expected total produced after 12 weeks.

3. Calculate the sum to infinity of the following series:

    a) 8, -1 , ⅛, ...
    b) $\frac{8}{3} + \frac{4}{9} + \frac{2}{27}$ ....
    c) $5 - 1 + \frac{1}{5}$............

4. A machine valued at K12 500 000, with a six year life, is estimated to have a scrap value of K450 000. If depreciation rate is 8%, find the depreciation charge per annum (Hint: use GP formula)

5. Find the sum of the first 20 terms of an arithmetic series whose first term a = -7, and common difference, d, is 3.5.

    b) Find the sum of the first 7 terms of the series:

        i)   4, 16, 64,-------------------
        ii)   3, 1, ⅓,.--------------------

6. a) Mrs. Clerk has been offered a job as a bank teller which pays a starting salary of K6 600 000 a year and a guaranteed annual raise of K450 000. How much will she earn during:

        i)   the third year?
        ii)   the seventh year?
        iii)   the twelfth year?

    c) Find Mrs. Clerk's total earnings for the first ten years if she will be at this job.

    d) Suppose Mrs. Clerk has the option of taking an annual raise of 4% (of her preceding year's salary) instead of the fixed annual raise of K450 000. Which option would be more profitable so far as her total? earnings for the first twelve years are concerned?

7. a) Mr. Caring Father opened a savings account for his son by depositing K100   000 on the day he was born, and on each subsequent birthday he deposited K20 000 more than the year before. How much did he deposit on:

        i)   his son's seventh birthday
        ii)   his son's tenth birthday
        iii)   his son's fifteenth birthday

    b) Find Mr. Caring Father's total deposit (not counting interest) after he has just   made the deposit on his son's fifteenth birthdays.

8. A national sports bureau service ranks football teams by asking 35 prominent coaches to list whichever teams they consider to be first, second, third, ... and tenth.   To combine these ratings the bureau service awards 10 points for a first place vote, 9 points for a second,- place vote, 8 points for a third – place vote,........... and 1 point for a tenth- place vote. What is the total number of points awarded to all the teams?

9. A bank's non-performing loans totaled K1, 527,000,000 in 1994 and K2, 040,000,000 in 2003. If the bank's non-performing loans increased by the same amount each year, what is this amount, and what were the overall combined non-performing loans for the years 1994 through 2003.

10. Find the simple rule or formula which characterizes each of the following progressions and write down the next three terms.

    a)   0, 2, 5, 7, 10, 12, 15,...

    b)   128, ⁻64, 32, ⁻16, 8, ⁻4, ...

    c)   3, 9, 37, 81, 243,...

    d) $\frac{1}{3}, \frac{1}{5}, \frac{1}{7}, \frac{1}{9},$ ....

    e) $1, \frac{5}{2}, 4, \frac{11}{2}, 7, \frac{17}{2}, 10,$..

    f)   1, 2, 4, 7, 11, 16, 22, 29,...

CHAPTER 5

BINOMIAL THEOREM

A binomial is a mathematical expression involving two terms, connected by plus or minus ($^+$ or $^-$).Examples are (a) $a + b$,   (b) $x^2 - y^2$ (c) $x^n \pm y^m$
 in mathematics it is quite tedious to multiply expressions such as $(x + y)^n$, $n \geq 2$.

In trying to search for a formula to simplify such expressions, we begin by considering the following:

$(x - y)^n$. i.e. $(x, y \neq 0)$

For n = 0 $(x + y)^0 = 1$

   n = 1 $(x + y) = x + y$

   n = 2 $(x + y)^2 = x^2 + 2xy + y^2$

   n = 3 $(x + y)^3 = x^3 + 3x^2y + 3x^2y + y^3$

   n = 4 $(x + y)^4 = x^4 + 4x^3y + 4x^2y^2 + 4xy^3$

Rules

In the above expansion the following rules are to applied.

1. The first term is x^n and the last y^n
2. The powers of x decrease by 1 from left to right while the powers of y increase by 1 from left to right
3. The powers of x and y for any particular term add up to n
4. The number of terms is given by n + 1.

PASCAL'S TRIANGLE
The number of combinations of r objects selected from a set of n objects, namely, the binomial coefficients can be determined by means of the following arrangement called Pascal's Triangle.

Rule: '*Each row begins with a 1, ends with a 1, and each other entry is the sum of the nearest two entries in the row immediately above* '

The above binomial expression can be written in terms of binominal coefficients as:

$(x + y)^0 = 1$

$(x + y)^1 = 1 \ \ 1$

$(x + y)^2 = 1 \ \ 2 \ \ 1$

$(x + y)^3 = 1 \ \ 3 \ \ 3 \ \ 1$

$(x + y)^4 = 1 \quad 4 \quad 6 \quad 4 \quad 1$

$(x + y)^5 = 1 \quad 5 \quad 10 \quad 10 \quad 5 \quad 1$

Pascal's Triangle

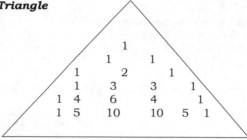

Example 1

Expand the following using binomial expansion.

   a) $(a + b)^4$

   b) $\left(x + \dfrac{1}{x} \right)^5$

Solution

   a) $(a + b)^4 = 1a^3b1 + 6a^2b^2 + 4a^1b^3 + 4a^0b^4 + 1a^4b^0$

$$= a^4 + a^3b + 6a^2b^2 + 4ab^3 + b^4$$

b) $\left(x + \dfrac{1}{x} \right)^5 = 1x^5 \left(\dfrac{1}{x} \right)^0 + 5x^4 \left(\dfrac{1}{x} \right)^1 + 10x^3 \left(\dfrac{1}{x} \right)^2$

$$+ 10x^2 \left(\dfrac{1}{x} \right)^3 + 5x \left(\dfrac{1}{x} \right)^4 + 1x^0 \left(\dfrac{1}{x} \right)^5$$

$$= x^5 + 5x^4 \left(\dfrac{1}{x} \right) + 10x^3 \left(\dfrac{1}{x} \right) + 10x^2 \left(\dfrac{1}{x^2} \right) + 5x \left(\dfrac{1}{x^4} \right) + \left(\dfrac{1}{x^5} \right)$$

$$= x^4 + 5x^3 + 10x + 10 \left(\dfrac{1}{x} \right) + 5 \left(\dfrac{1}{x^3} \right) + \left(\dfrac{1}{x^5} \right)$$

BINOMIAL THEOREM DERIVATION

Theorem states that for any positive integer,

$$(x + y)^n = \binom{n}{0} x^n + \binom{n}{1} x^{n-1} y + \binom{n}{2} x^{n-2} y^2 + \binom{n}{3} x^{n-3} y^3$$

$$-------- + \binom{n}{n-1} x^n y^{n-1} + \binom{n}{n} y^n$$

$$= \sum_{r=0}^{n} \binom{n}{r} x^{n-r} y^r$$

From above expansion we note the following:

1. Each term is of the form $\binom{n}{r} x^{n-r} y^r$.

2. The value of r for the Kth term is given by r = K – 1 e.g. the third term is r = 3 – 1 = 2.

Note that binomial theorem is derived from combinatorial mathematics.

Thus, $\binom{n}{r} = {}^nC_r = \dfrac{n!}{(n-r)\,!r!}$

Remember:

1! = 1

0! = 1

n! = n (n -1) !

The binomial calculated earlier can be presented as:

$(x + y)^0 = 1 = \binom{0}{0}$

$(x + y)^1 = 1 \ 1 = \binom{1}{0} \binom{1}{1}$

$(x + y)^2 = 2 \ \ 21 = \binom{2}{0} \binom{2}{1} \binom{2}{2}$

$(x + y)^3 = 1 \ 3 \ 3 \ 1 = \binom{3}{0} \binom{3}{1} \binom{3}{2} \binom{3}{3}$

From above we see that the expansion

$(x + y)^3 = x^3 + 3x^2y + 3xy^2 + y^3$

$$= \binom{3}{0} x^3 + \binom{3}{1} x^2y + \binom{3}{2} xy + \binom{3}{3} y^3$$

Example 2

In the expansion of $\left(x + \dfrac{1}{x}\right)^4$, find the third term

Solution

In binomial expansion, each term is given by $\binom{n}{r} a^{n-r} b^r$

From the binomial above $n = 4$, $r = 3-1 = 2$, $a = x$, $b = \dfrac{1}{x}$

Required expansion is:

$$\binom{4}{2} x^{4-2} \;,\; \left(\frac{1}{x}\right)^2$$

$$= \binom{4}{2} \cdot x^2 \cdot \frac{1}{x^2}$$

$$= \binom{4}{2} = \frac{4!}{(4-2)!\,2!} = \frac{4!}{2!2!} = 6$$

The third term is $\underline{6}$

Confirmation:

$$\left(x + \frac{1}{x}\right)^4 = x^4 + 4x^3.\frac{1}{x} + 6x^2.\frac{1}{x^2} + 4x.\frac{1}{x^3} + \frac{1}{x^4}$$

$$= x^4 + 4x^2 + \underline{6} + 4\frac{1}{x^2} + \frac{1}{x^4}$$

Alternatively $\left(x + \dfrac{1}{x}\right)^4$ can be expanded using

$$(a+b)^n = a^n + \frac{na^{n-1}b}{1!} + \frac{n(n-1)a^{n-2}b^2}{2!} + \frac{n(n-1)(n-2)a^{n-3}b^3}{3!}$$

$\left(x + \dfrac{1}{x}\right)^4$, $a = x$, $b = \dfrac{1}{x}$, $n = 4$

$$x^4 + \frac{4(x)^3\left(\frac{1}{x}\right)}{1!} + \frac{3(4)(x)^2\left(\frac{1}{x}\right)^2}{2!} + \frac{2(3)(4)(x)\left(\frac{1}{x}\right)^3}{3!}$$

$$+ \frac{1(2)(x)^3\left(\frac{1}{x}\right)^4}{4!}$$

$$= x^4 + 4x^2 + \frac{12}{2} + \frac{24}{6}\left(\frac{1}{x}\right)^2 + \frac{24}{24}\left(\frac{1}{x}\right)^4$$

$$= x^4 + 4x^2 + \underline{6} + 4 \left(\frac{1}{x}\right)^2 + \left(\frac{1}{x}\right)^4$$

Thus, the third term is 6 as found before.

Example 3

Expand and simplify $(1.05)^5$ to 5 decimal places.

Solution

$(1.05)^5 = (1 + 0.05)$, a = 1, b = 0.05, n = 5

$$\frac{1^5 (1)^4 (0.05)}{1!} + \frac{4 (5) (1)^3 (0.05)^2}{2!} + \frac{3 (4) (5) (1^2 (0.05)^3}{3!} + \frac{2 (3) (4) (5) (1) (0.05)^4}{3!}$$

$$+ \frac{1 (2) (3) (4) (5) (0.05)^5}{5!}$$

$$= 1 + \frac{0.25}{1} + \frac{0.05}{2} + \frac{0.0075}{6} + \frac{0.0075}{24} + \frac{0.0000375}{120}$$

$$= 1 + 0.25 + 0.025 + 0.00125 + 0.00003125 + 0.000000312$$

$$= 1.276281562$$

$$= 1.27628 \text{ to 5 decimal places.}$$

Note: workout the number in brackets raised and then multiply by approximate numbers. The order of operation is key here and it must be observed.

Example 4

Expand and simplify $(3x + 2y)^5$

Solution

$(3x + 2y) 5$, a = 3x, b = 2y, n = 5

$$\frac{(3x) + 5 (3x)^4 (2y)}{1!} + \frac{4(5) (3x)^3 (2y)^2}{2!} + \frac{3 (4) (5) (3x)^2 (2y)^3}{3!} + \frac{2 (3) (4) (5) (3x) (2y)}{5!}$$

$$+ \frac{5 (81x 4) (2y)}{1} + \frac{4 (5) 27x^3) (4y^2)}{2} + \frac{60 (9x 2) (8y 3)}{6} + \frac{120 (3x) 16y 4)}{24}$$

$$+ \frac{120(32y 5)}{120}$$

$= 243x^5 + 810xy + 1080x3y^2 + 720x2y^3 + 240xy^4 + 32y^5$

Note: One common mistake students make is to forget that a = 3x multiply that both 3 and x must be raised to the power n. Further, note that the rules stated earlier own are followed fully and this provides a way of checking the corrections of your answers. Be alert and don't fall into the mathematical trap!

THE BINOMIAL THEOREM AND NEGATIVE POWERS

Binomial theorem can be used for negative powers just as positive powers. The rules are the same as illustrated by the following examples.

Example 5

Simplify $(1.05)^{-5}$ to 5 decimal places

Solution

$(1.05)^{-5} = (1 + 0.05)^{-5}$, a = 1, b= 0.05, n = -5

$$\frac{1^{-5} + (-5)(1)^{-6}(0.05) + (-6)(-5)(1)^{-7}(0.05)^2 + (-7)(-6)(1)^{-8}(0.05)8}{4! \qquad\qquad 2! \qquad\qquad 3!}$$

$$+ \frac{(-8)(-7)(-6)(-5)(1)^{-9}(0.05)^4 + (-9)(-8)(-7)(-6)(-5)(1)^{-10}(0.050)^5}{4! \qquad\qquad 5!}$$

$$= 1 - 0.25 + \frac{0.075}{2} - 0.02625 + \frac{0.0105}{24} = \frac{0,00472}{120}$$

$$= -0.000039375$$

$$= 0.783523125$$

$$= \underline{0.78352}$$

Example 6

Expand $(3x + 2y)^{-5}$

Solution

$(3x + 2y)^{-5}$, a = 3x, b = 2y, n = -5

$$\frac{(3x)^{-5} + (-5)3x)^{-6}(2y) + (-6)(-5)(3x)^{-7}(2y)^2 + (-7)(-6)(-5)(3x)^{-8}(2y)^3}{1! \qquad\qquad 2! \qquad\qquad 3!}$$

$$+ \frac{(-8)(-7)(-6)(-5)(3x)^{-9}(2y)^4 + (-9)(-8)(-7)(-6)(-5)(3x)^{-10}(2y)^5}{4! \qquad\qquad 5!}$$

$$= 0.004115226x^{-5} - 0.013717421x^{-6}y + \frac{0.05486984x^{-7}y^2}{2} - \frac{0.25058523x^{-8}y^3}{6}$$

$$+ \frac{1.365645456x^{-9}y^4}{24} - \frac{8.193872736y^5}{120}$$

$$= 0.004115226x^{-5} - 0.013717421x^{-6}y + 0.027434842x^{-7}y^2 - 0.04267242x^{-8}y^3$$

$$+ 0.056901894x^{-9}y^4 - 0.068282272y^5.$$

Note: Again the rules governing binomial theorem are fully applied.

BINOMIAL THEOREM AND POSITIVE FRACTIONAL POWERS

The same rules apply as illustrated by the following example.

Example 7

Evaluate $(1.03)^{3/2}$ to five decimal places

Solution

$(1.03)^{3/2} = (1 + 0.03)^{3/2}$, $a = 1$, $b = 0.03$, $n = 3/2$

Using $(a + b)^n = \dfrac{a^n + na^{n-1}b}{1!} + \dfrac{n(n-1)a^{n-2}b^2}{2!} + \dfrac{n(n-1)a^{n-3}b^3}{3!} + \ldots\ldots$

$$\frac{1^{3/2} + (3/2)(1)^{1/2}(0.03)}{1!} + \frac{(1/2)(3/2)(1)^{-1/2}(0.03)^2}{2!} + \frac{(-1/2)(1/2)(3/2)(1)^{-3/}(0.03)^3}{3!}$$

$$+ \frac{(-3/2)(-1/2)(1/2)(3/2)(1)^{-5/2}(0.03)^4}{4!} + \ldots\ldots\ldots$$

$= 1 + 0.045 + 0.0003375 - 0.000001687 + 0.000000018$

$= 1.000335832$

$= 1.00034$ to five decimal places

Note: 1 raised to any number gives 1. Since the answer required is in decimal form, you can convert the fractions in decimal so as to enable you use the calculator quickly. For example, $3/2 = 1.5$, $1/2 = 0.5$, etc.

BINOMIAL THEOREM AND NEGATIVE FRACTIONAL POWERS

The same rules apply. Check the following example.

Example 8

Evaluate $(1.03)^{-3/2}$ to five decimal places

Solution

$(1.03)^{-3/2} = (1 + 0.03)^{-3/2}$, $a = 1$, $b = 0.03$, $n = -3/2$.

Using $(a + b)^n = \dfrac{a^n + na^{n-1}b}{1!} + \dfrac{n(n-1)a^{n-2}b^2}{2!} + \dfrac{n(n-1)(n-2)a^{n-3}b^3}{3!}$

$1^{-3/2} + \dfrac{(-3/2)(1)^{-5/2}(0.03)}{1!} + \dfrac{(-5/2)(-3/2)(1)^{-7/2}(0.03)^2}{2!}$

$+ \dfrac{(-7/2)(-5/2)(-3/2)(1)^{-9/2}(0.03)^3}{3!} + \dfrac{(-9/2)(-7/2)(-5/2)(-3/2)(1)^{-11/2}(0.03)^4}{4!} + ...$

$= 1 - 0.045 + 0.0016875 - 0.0000590625 + 0.00000199$

$= 0.956630427$

$= 0.95663$ to 5 decimal places.

Note: When you have negative fractional power it becomes difficult to determine when to end your series. The guide to follow is to look at the required number of decimal places for your final answer.

- 1 raised to any number will equal 1 whether negative or positive. Further, working with fractional powers can be fast and interesting as soon as you are able to find a pattern. Specifically, in the above we have just been adding -2 to each preceding numerator of the fractional power to get the next power while maintaining the denominator of 2. Learn the pattern to quicken your calculations!

ADDENDUM: PARTIAL FRACTIONS

The process of decomposing or splitting a given rational number into two or more rational functions is caked partial fractions. This can be achieved by using elimination or comparing coefficients method for a linear function. The first step is to determine whether you have a proper or improper fraction before resolving. Detailed discussion on partial fractions is beyond the tenets of this book. Only the basics are given here.

Example 9

Resolve $\dfrac{x^4}{x^2 - 9}$ into partial fractions.

Solution

Above is an improper fraction.

$$\begin{array}{r}
x^2 - 9 \\
x^2 - 9 \overline{\smash{\big)}\ x^4 + 0x^2} \\
\underline{-\ x^4 - 9x^2} \\
-9x^2 + 0 \\
\underline{9x^2 - 81} \\
81
\end{array}$$

Thus, $\dfrac{x^4}{x^2 - 9} = x^2 - 9$ remainder 81

Notes:

1. The fraction is improper because the power of the numerator is greater than the power of the denominator.

2. First we divided x^2 into x^4 which gives us x^2

3. Next we multiply x^2 by $x^2 - 9$ to get $x^4 - 9x^2$

4. Next we subtract $x^4 - 9x^2$ from $x^4 + 0x^2$. The $0x^2$ is simply put for normal presentation.

5. Next we divide x^2 into $-9x^2$ which gives -9 and then we multiply -9 by $x^2 - 9$ which gives $9x^2 - 81$ and then subtract $9x^2 - 81$ from $-9x^2 + 0$ to get 81 which is a remainder.

Example 10

Find the first four terms of the quotient $\dfrac{1}{1 + x}$ by dividing into 1.

Solution

$$\begin{array}{r}
1 - x + x^2 - x^3 \\
1 + x \overline{\smash{\big)}\ 1 + 0x} \\
\underline{-\ 1 + x} \\
-x \\
\underline{(-x - x^2)} \\
x^2 \\
\underline{-\ (x^2 + x^3)} \\
-x^3 \\
\underline{(-x^3 - x^4)} \\
x^4
\end{array}$$

Thus, the first four terms of $\dfrac{1}{1 + x} = 1 - x + x^2 - x^3$. Prove the answer by using

The binomial theorem to expand $(1 + x)^{-1}$.

PROGRESS CLINIC 5

i)   Expand $(a + b)^9$

ii)   By using Pascal's Triangle principles determine the coefficients of $(a + b)^n$ when (a) n = 5, (b) n = 7 (c) n = 9

iii)   Use the binomial theorem to expand each of the following and simplify as much as possible:

(a) $(1 + 3x)^3$ (b) $(2x + 3y)^4$ (c) $(5x - 2)^6$.

iv)   Using the first four terms of appropriate binomial expansions, find approximate values of:
(a) $(1.03)^8$ (b) $(1.05)^{10}$

v)   Write 0.98 as $1 - 0.02$ and use the first three terms of the corresponding binomial expansion to find the approximate value of $(0.98)^6$.

vi)   To consider a practical application of the binomial theorem, suppose that we are investing K5000 000 in a savings certificate paying 8% compounded quarterly and want to know much this investment will be worth 10 years hence.

a.   Use ordinary compounding principles
b.   Use binomial expansion of $(1 + 0.2)^{40}$ (Note: use first four terms only).
c.   How different are the two answers and what would happen if we used three more terms of the expansion

vii)   Evaluate:

a. $(1.03)^{-3/2}$ to 5 decimal places
b. $(1.03)^{3/2}$ to 6 decimal places
c. $(2x + 3y)^{3/2}$ to first four terms
d. $(2x + 3y)^{-3/2}$ to first four terms

viii)   Resolve the following into partial fractions:

a. $\dfrac{x^3}{x^2 - 1}$

b. $(1 + x)^{-1}$

CHAPTER 6

COMPOUNDING AND DISCOUNTING

INTRODUCTION

At times, all of us find it convenient to save money. Some very fortunate people cannot help but save as their expenditure is less than their income! There are many reasons why an individual may save money.

If an individual invests money, he will want to make a financial return. For the investor, interest is the amount of money which an investment earns, when it is invested for a certain length of time. For the borrower, interest is the amount of money paid for using other people's money.

In this chapter, we take a look at computations involving simple interest, compounding and discounting.

SIMPLE INTEREST

This is interest which is earned in equal amount every year or month and which is a given proportion of the original investment or the principal.

If a sum of money is invested for a period of time, then the amount of simple interest which accrues is equal to number of accounting period x interest rate x amount invested.

$$I = nrP$$

Where I = simple interest
      P = principal amount
      n = number of years
       r = interest rate expressed as a proportion

Note that in the above formula nrp is the interest earned.

Thus, the terminal value (s) is given by

$$S = P + I \quad \text{or} \quad S = P + nrP \quad \text{or} \quad S = P(1 + nr)$$

Above formula can be used to calculate the value of any variable provided that the values of the three other variables are known.

Alternatively, simple interest formula may be presented as

$$I = \frac{PTR}{100}$$

Where I = interest
      P = principal
      T = number of years
       R = interest rate expressed as a percentage

Interest earned per year = $\dfrac{\text{Total Interest Earned}}{\text{Number of years}}$

Example 1

A customer has deposited K1000 000 in a savings account that gives 10% simple interest per annum.

(a)   Calculate the interest earned per year.
(b)   Calculate interest earned per month
(c)   Calculate the total amount in the account at the end of the 5th year.

Solution

a)   Simple interest (I) = nrp
      Where p = K1000 000
          n = 5 years
          r = 0.1

      I = K1000 000 X 5 X 0.1

       = K500 000

b)   Interest per year = $\dfrac{\text{Total interest earned}}{\text{Number of years}}$

              = $\dfrac{\text{K500 000}}{\text{5 years}}$

              = K100 000 per year

Therefore, interest per month = $\dfrac{\text{Interest per year}}{\text{Number of months per year}}$

              = $\dfrac{\text{K100 000}}{\text{12 months}}$

              = K8 333.33 per month

Note that we could get the same result by simply dividing the interest earned in 5 years by the number of months in 5 years which is 60.

i.e. $\dfrac{\text{K500 000}}{\text{5 X 12 months}}$ = $\dfrac{\text{K500 000}}{\text{60 months}}$ = K8 333.33

c) Total amount which is also called the terminal value is calculated using the following formula.

$S = P + nrp$

$= K1000\ 000 + 5 \times 0.1 \times K1000\ 000$

$= K1000\ 000 + K500\ 000$

$= \underline{K1,\ 500,\ 000}$.

Alternatively, $S = P\ (1 + nr)$

$= K1000\ 000\ \left[1 + (5 \times 0.1) \right]$

$= K1000\ 000\ (1.5)$

$= \underline{K1,500,\ 000\ \text{as before}}$

Example 2

Mr. Savings has an account with a local bank where he invests K160 000 on 1st January each year in which simple interest is credited at 12% on 31st December. This interest is put in a separate account and does not itself earn interest.

Find the total amount standing to his credit on 31st December following his 5th payment of K160 000.

Solution

We can approach the above problem using a schedule to show how both the investment and interest are changing as at 1st January and 31st December.

Year (1 January)	Investment	interest	31st December
1	K160 000	$\dfrac{12}{100} \times 160\ 000$	K19 200
2	160 000 + 160 000	$\dfrac{12}{100} \times 320\ 000$	38 400
3	320 000 + 160 000	$\dfrac{12}{100} \times 480$	57 600
4	480 000 + 160 000	$\dfrac{12}{100} \times 640\ 000$	76 800
5	640 000 + 160 000	$\dfrac{12}{100} \times 800\ 000$	96 000
		Total	K288 000

Total amount on 31ˢᵗ December following the 5ᵗʰ payment is:

S = P + I

  = K800 000 + K288 000

  = <u>K1,088,000</u>

Note that interest figures as at 31ˢᵗ December for each year is calculated using the same formula I = nrp or I = $\frac{PTR}{100}$

TAKING A DETOUR IN SIMPLE INTEREST CALCULATIONS

The examples above illustrated straight forward computations of simple interest because we were using the number of years. However, in practice, banks use "days" or "months" in computing simple interest than "years". Now in a clear year, there are 365 days except in a leap year, when we have 366 days. Additionally, there are 12 months in a year with differing days: some months have 30 days, others 31 days and February has 28 days and 29 days in a leap year.

Now the calculation of simple interest will differ depending on whether we are using a 360-day year i.e. 12 months each with 30 days or 365-days i.e. 12 months each with 30, 31 and 28 days as the case may be. Additionally, time used whether exact or approximate also affects the computations. Let's now take a look at this deviation with examples.

EXACT AND ORDINARY SIMPLE INTEREST

- Exact interest is calculated on the basis of exact number of days in a year. For most of the years 365 days is used.

- Ordinary simple interest, on the other hand, is calculated on the basis of 360-days year. Of the two, ordinary simple interest is preferred as it simplifies most computations apart from the fact that it increases interest collected by the lender of money.

Example 3

Find the exact and ordinary simple interest on K5000 000 for 30 days at 6%

Solution

The equation I = nrp is still the one applicable here though we now use the days for n.

We have p = K5000 000

       r = 0.06

For exact simple interest, we use 365 day year.

Thus, I = K5000 000 X 0.06 X $\left[\frac{30 \text{ days}}{365 \text{ days}} \right]$

$$= \text{K5000 000} \times 0.06 \times \frac{6}{73}$$

$$= \text{K5000 000} \times 0.06 \times \frac{6}{73} \times 6$$

$$= \text{K24, 657. 53425}$$

$$\underline{= \text{K24, 657.53}}$$

Note we always first divide the numerator and denominator for n by 5 to always have $\frac{1}{73}$ by conversion

For ordinary simple interest, we use 360-days year

Thus, I = n r p

$$= \text{K5000 000} \times 0.06 \times \left(\frac{30 \text{ days}}{360 \text{ days}} \right)$$

$$= \text{K5000 000} \times 0.06 \times \frac{1}{12}$$

$$\underline{= \text{K25, 000}}$$

This confirms the fact that ordinary simple interest increases the interest collected by the lender of money when compared to the exact simple interest.

Example 4

Show that exact simple interest is the same as the ordinary simple interest decreased by $\frac{1}{73}$ of itself.

Solution

Have you seen the reason why I mentioned that we need to convert figures so that we end up with $\frac{1}{73}$ when computing exact simple interest? Well, I hope you do now.

To show that exact simple interest is the same as the ordinary simple interest decreased by $\frac{1}{73}$ of itself, we start by taking exact simple to be Ie and ordinary Simple interest to be Io and n the number of days interest is earned.

Using I = n r P

We have $Ie = Pr \left(\frac{n}{365} \right) = \frac{Prn}{365}$

$$Io = Pr \left(\frac{n}{360}\right) = \frac{Prn}{360}$$

$$= \frac{Prn}{365} \times \frac{360}{Prn}$$

$$= \frac{72}{73}$$

From $\dfrac{Ie}{Io} = \dfrac{72}{73}$

$$= 73Ie = 72Io$$

Making Ie the subject of the formula we have $Ie = \dfrac{72}{73} Io$

Taking the whole to be 1, we decrease this 1 by $\dfrac{1}{73}$ to give us:

$$Ie = \left(1 - \frac{1}{73}\right) Io$$

Substituting Ie above for Io we have $Ie = Io - \dfrac{1}{73} Io$ as the required proof.

Note that any number could be used to provide the proof but 1 is preferred since $\dfrac{1}{73}$ is a fraction.

EXACT AND APPROXIMATE TIME

When days are given, the number of days for which interest is calculated becomes very important. The number of days can be found in two ways namely:

- Exact time which is the exact number of days as found from the calendar.

  Thus, required number of days is equal to the number of days remaining in the month plus number of days in the next months plus indicated number of days in the last month. Alternatively, the table of calendar days is used to determine exact time. When using this table always ADD 365 when two different years are involved and ADD 1 when a leap year is involved before subtracting.

- Approximate time, on the other hand, is found by assuming that each month has 30 days.

Example 5

Find the exact and approximate time from 20th June 2006 to 24th August 2006

Solution

- For exact time, the required number of days is equal to number of days remaining in June plus the number of days in July plus the indicated number of days in August.

Thus, 10 + 31 + 24 = 65

- This could be determined from tables where 20th June is numbered 171 and 24th August is numbered 236. The required number of days is 236 – 171 = 65 as before.

- For the approximate time, we set our working as follows: by changing the actual month into the month number in the year.

August 24, 2006   as   2006 : 8 : 24
June   30, 2006   as   2006 : 6 : 20
                                  0 : 2 : 4

After subtracting the approximate time is 2 months and 4 days or 64 days assuming a 30-day month.

Example 7

Find the exact time and approximate time from 20th June to 24th August of the following year.

Solution

Exact time:

August 24   236
Add 365 for extending into another year   +365
                                         601
June 20   - 171
                                  430 days

Approximate time:

Assume the two years to be 2010 and 2011'

August 24, 2011   as   2011: 08: 24
June 20, 20 10   as   2010: 06: 20
                     01 : 02 :04 i.e.1 year 2 months and 4 days=424 days.

THE FOUR RULES OF SIMPLE INTEREST

The four rules of simple interest represent a combination of exact and ordinary simple interest with exact and approximate time as illustrated in the following example.

Example 8

Find the exact and ordinary interest on K20 000 000 at 9% from 20th April 2006 to 1st July 2006 using exact time and approximate time.

Solution

This question combines exact and approximate time with exact and ordinary interest.

- Exact time = 11 + 31 + 30 = 72 days.

- Approximate time

$$2006 : 7 : 1$$
$$\underline{2006 : 4 : 20}$$
$$\underline{0 : 2 : 11}$$

Which is 2 months 11 days or 71 days assuming a 30-day month.

- Exact interest using exact time

$$I = K20\ 000\ 000\ (0.09)\left(\frac{72}{360}\right)$$

$$= \underline{K355,\ 068.49832}$$

- Exact interest using approximate time

$$I = K20\ 000\ 000\ (0.09)\left(\frac{71}{365}\right) = K25,560,000 \times 1 = \underline{K350,136.9863}$$

- Ordinary interest using exact time

$$I = K20\ 000\ 000\ (0.09)\left(\frac{72}{360}\right) = \underline{K360,\ 000}$$

- Ordinary interest using approximate time

$$I = K20\ 000\ 000\ (0.09)\left(\frac{71}{360}\right) = \underline{K355,000}$$

Critical examination of the answers to the above example reveals that the highest interest is earned from ordinary interest for the exact number of days. As such it is the most popular among commercial bank hence it is also called the **Bankers Rule**.

Example 9

Jacob borrowed k9 600 000 on September 12 to start college. He repaid the loan on 12th August of the following year. What amount did he pay back if the bank calculated the exact interest at 14% and used exact time.

Solution

Exact time:
August 22   224
Add   +365
                 589
September12   - 255
                 334

I = Prn

 K9 600 000 x 0.14x334/365= K1,229,852.05

S = P + I

S = k9 600 000 + k 1 229, 852.05 = k10,829,852.05. This is the amount he paid back.

Example 10

Jacob borrowed k9 600 000 on September 12 to start college. He repaid the loan on August 22 the following year. What amount did he pay back if the bank calculated the ordinary simple interest at 14% and used exact time?

Solution

Exact time is 334 day as calculated in example 9 above.

I = Prn

I = k9 600 000x0.14x334/360 = k1, 246,933.33

S = P+I

S = k9 600 000 + k 1 246 933.33 = k10, 846, 933.33. This being the amount he paid back.

Example 11

Use the banker's rule to find Simple interest on k56 500 000 at 33¼% from February 18 to May 4 of the same leap year.

Solution

Exact Time:

May 4	124
Add	+_1_ for leap year
	125
February 18	- 49
	76 days

I = k56 500 000x0.3325x76/365 = k3,911, 657.49

APPLICATION OF SIMPLE INTEREST: PROMISSORY NOTE

- One most common application of simple interest computations is to be found in transactions involving promissory notes.

- A promissory note is a written promise by a debtor to pay to, or to the order of the creditor a specified sum of money on a specified date. A promissory note could be with or without interest.

- From the above definition of a promissory note, the following features must be identified:

1. It has a *term* which is the period in months or days explicitly stated in the note.

2. It has a *face value* which is the amount stated in the note.

3. It has *maturity value* which is the amount to be paid on the maturity date.

4. *Maturity date* which is the date on which the debt is to be paid.

The above salient features of a promissory note can be presented diagrammatically as follows.

K5 000 000	Mazabuka, April 15, 2007

Three months after date I promise to pay to

the order of PCBF Limited

five million and 00/100 Kwachas

at Plot 685, Cairo Road, Lusaka.

Value received with interest at 18%

No. Due December 15, 2007   Sikily Mwiinga

Generally, maturity value and face value for a non-interest bearing promissory note are the same. However, the maturity value is always greater than the face value for interest bearing promissory note. Maturity date of a promissory note is found using approximate time if the term is given in months and exact time if the term is given in days.

To obtain maturity value of a note ordinary simple interest is normally used.

Example 12

Using the promissory note above 'determine.

a)   The debtor
b)   The creditor
c)   The term
d)   Maturity date
e)   Maturity value

Solution

a) the debtor is Sikily Mwiinga
b) the creditor is PCBF Limited
c) the term is three months
d) maturity or due date is December 15, 2007
e) maturity value is K5 000 000 + K5 000 000 X 0.18 X $\frac{3}{12}$

K5 000 000 + K225 000

= <u>K5, 225,000</u>

Note that maturity value is calculated using S = P + Prn or S = P + I

APPLICATION OF SIMPLE DISCOUNT: PROMISSORY NOTES

A promissory note is an IOU (I owe you) security which can be traded second hand. This means that a promissory note may be sold one or more times before its maturity date. Each buyer will have to discount the maturity value of the note for the time from the date of sale to the maturity date of his discount.

Example 13

Find the proceeds of the sale 10 months before due of 12 months note which is discounted at 5% and the value is to be received with interest at 3%. The face value of the note is K10 000 000.

Solution

To find the value of the proceeds we must first find the maturity value of the note at 3% interest and then discount for 10 months at 15%.

Here P = K10 000 000

r = 0.03

n = $\frac{10}{12}$

Using I = Prn

Interest = K10 000 000 X 0.03 X $\frac{12}{12}$

= K300 000

Maturity value = P + Prn or P (1 + rn)

= K10 000 000 + K300 000

= K10 300 000

Discount period is 10 months

Simple discount is Pdn

= K10 000 000 X 0.05 X $\frac{10}{12}$

= K416, 666.66

Proceeds = Maturity value Simple discount

= K10 300 000 – K416, 666.66

= K9 883 333.34

Thus, the buyer will have to pay K9 883 333.34 to obtain possession of the promissory note so as to receive K10 300 000 at maturity from the seller (if held to maturity).

PRESENT VALUE OF A DEBT

The present value of a debt is the value of a debt on some date prior to its maturity date.

The present value P at r simple interest on S maturity value due in n years is given as follows:

$$P = \frac{S}{1 + rn}$$ or P = S(1+rn)$^{-1}$

Where P = present value of a debt

S = maturity value of a debt

n = number of years

r = simple interest

Example 9

Find the present value of 10 % simple interest of K20 000 000 due in 7 months.

Solution

From above S = K20 000 000

$$n = \frac{7}{12}$$

$$r = 0.1$$

$$p = ?$$

Using $P = \dfrac{S}{1 + nr} = \dfrac{K20\ 000\ 000}{1 + 0.1\left(\dfrac{7}{12}\right)}$

$$= \frac{K20\ 000\ 000}{1.058333333}$$

$$= \underline{K18,\ 897,\ 637.80}$$

Sometimes, you face questions with two rates of interest and you may be wondering as to what should be dene in such a situation. The next example illustrates the technique.

Example 14

A promissory note dated April 10 for K20 000 000 due in 10 months with interest at 8% is sold on July 24 to Choolwe to whom money is worth 10%. How much does Choolwe pay for the note?

Solution

We first find the maturity value of the note and then find the present value of the maturity value so calculated.

Maturity value S = P (1 + rn)

Where p = K20 000 000

$$r = 0.08$$

$$n = \frac{10}{12}$$

Thus, $S = K20\ 000\ 000 \left[1 + 0.08\left(\dfrac{10}{12}\right)\right]$

$$= K20\ 000\ 000 \times 1.06666667$$

= $\underline{K21, 333, 333. 33}$

Present value of K21, 333, 333. 33 at 10% simple interest due in 140 (i.e. July 24 to December 10, the maturity date).

Using $P = \dfrac{S}{1 + rn}$

$$= \frac{K21, 333, 333.33}{1 + 0.1 \left(\dfrac{140}{360} \right)}$$

$$= \frac{K21, 333, 333. 33}{1.038888889}$$

$$= \underline{K20, 534,795.35}$$

EQUATIONS OF VALUE

Another area which requires our appreciation as far as simple interest is concerned has something to do with equations of value. In reality most transactions involving the debtor and creditor will require agreement on simple interest and on the evaluation date or the focal date.

Sometimes the debtor may wish to replace a set of his financial obligation by another set.

Example 15

Today John owes K1000 000 with interest for 1.5 years at 4% due in 6 months and K2 500 000 due in 9 months without interest. He wishes to pay K2 000 000 today and settle his obligations by a final payment 1 year from today. If money is worth 8% simple interest and the focal date is one year from today, find this payment.

Solution

The first thing to do is to calculate the maturity value of the interest bearing portion of debt as follows:

$S = P (1 + rn)$

$$= K1000\ 000 \left(1 + 0.04 \times \frac{9}{6} \right)$$

$$= K1000\ 000$$

$$= K1, 060,000$$

Letting x to denote the required payment, the information can be presented in a time line as follows:

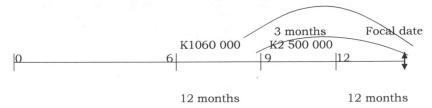

From above, we can evaluate each item as of the focal date and equating the sums of the values of the old and new obligations as shown below

K2 160 000 (1 + 0.08) + x = K1000 000 (1 +0.08 X ½) + K2 500 000 (1 + 0.08 X ¼)

K2 160 000 + x = K1102 400 + K2 550 000

K2 160 000 + x = K3 652 400

Thus, x = K1 492 400

Note that in the above calculation we used $\frac{6}{12}$ or ½ for n for K1060 000

Because the amount is half way to 12 months which is our focal date. In the same manner, we used $\frac{3}{12}$ or ¼ for n for K2 500 000 because the amount is three months away to 12 months.

Example 16

At 6% simple interest, find the value today of the following obligations: K1000 000 due today. K2 500 000 due in 6 months with interest at 10%, and K3500 000 due in 1 year with interest 8%.

        a) Using today as the focal date

        b) Using 1 year from today as the focal date.

Solution

a) Sum of the present values of the three obligations given as x is:

    K1000 000 due today

    $K2\ 500\ 000\left(1 + 0.1 \times \frac{6}{12}\right) = K2,625,000$ due in 6 months.

K3 500 000 $\left(1 + 0.08 \times \dfrac{12}{12}\right)$ = K3, 780,000 due in 1 year

This information can be presented using a time line as follows:

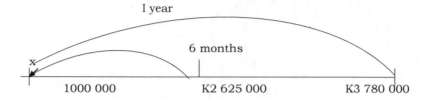

I year

6 months

x

1000 000   K2 625 000   K3 780 000

Now the sum of the present values of all these three obligations which is the value today of the obligations is:

x = K1000 000 + $\dfrac{K2\ 625\ 000}{\left(1 + 0.06 \times \dfrac{6}{12}\right)}$ + $\dfrac{K3\ 780\ 000}{\left(1 + 0.06 \times \dfrac{12}{12}\right)}$

= K1000 000 + $\dfrac{K2\ 625\ 000}{1.03}$ + $\dfrac{K3\ 780\ 000}{1.06}$

= K1000 000 + K2548 543.689 + K3 566 0.37. 736

= K7, 114, 581.43

b) Using 1 year from today as a focal date, the time line changes to the following:

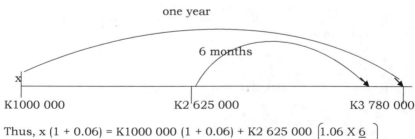

one year

6 months

x

K1000 000   K2 625 000   K3 780 000

Thus, x (1 + 0.06) = K1000 000 (1 + 0.06) + K2 625 000 $\left[1.06 \times \dfrac{6}{12}\right]$ + K3 780 000

x (1.06) = K1000 000 (1.06) + K2 625 000 (1.06 X 0.5) + K3780 000

x (1.06) = K1060 000 + K2,703,750

x (1.06) = K7,543,750

$x = \dfrac{K7, 43,750}{1.06}$

$= K7, 116,745.283$

$= \underline{K7, 116,745.28}$

Note, we have used the same data but different focal dates and have got different solutions. Thus, the value of x varies with the choice of the focal date. Therefore, it is important that you understand the focal date before performing any computations.

We can now take a "commercial Break" and when we come back we look at compound interest.

COMPOUNDING

Interest is normally calculated by mean of compounding. If a sum of money, the principal is put into a savings account at a fixed rate of interest such that

interest is added to the principal and no withdraws are made, then the amount deposited will grow at an increasing rate as time progresses because interest earned in earlier periods will earn interest in later periods.

We can compare simple interest and compound on a year by year basis by using a schedule as given in the example below.

Example 17

Find the total interest earned on K250 000 invested for 4 years at 8% interest using

   a) simple interest
   b) compound interest

Solution

		Simple interest		Compound interest
Year	Deposit	Interest	Deposit	Interest
1	250 000	250 000 X 0.08 = 20 000	250 000	250 000 X 0.08 = 20 000
2	250 000	250 000 X 0.08 = 20 000	270 000	270 000 X 0.08 = 21 600
3	250 000	250 000 X 0.08 = 20 000	291 600	291 600 X 0.08 = 23 382
4	250 000	250 000 X 0.08 = 20 000	314 928	3 14 928 X 0.08 = 25 194
		Total interest earned = k80 000		k90122.24

So we see that there is considerable difference between the two methods.

DERIVING THE COMPOUND INTEREST FORMULA

The value of deposit at the end of year is equal to value of deposit at beginning of year plus interest earned during the year.

Value of the deposit at end of first year = $P + rP$

(deposit at start)   (interest)

$$= P(1 + r) \text{ by factoring out } P.$$

Value of deposit at the end of 2nd year $= P(1 + r) + rP(P(1 + r)$

$$= (1 + r)(P + Pr)$$

$$= (1 + r)P(1 + r)$$

$$= P(1 + r)^2$$

Value of deposit at end of 3rd year $= P(1 + r)^2 + rP(1 + r)$

$$= (1 + r)^2(P + rP)$$

$$= (1 + r)^2 P(1 + r)$$

$$= P(1 + r)^3$$

So if we call S the value of the deposit after n years, then S for any number of years at a given rate and deposit can be found by using the following formula.

$$S = P(1 + r)^n$$

Where S = Sum available or future value
P = Principal or present value
n = Number of years
r = Interest rate

Total interest earned can be calculated using the following formula.

$$\text{Total interest: } P(1 + r)^n - P$$

Example 18

Using the same data of example 17, calculate the total interest earned and the amount available for the deposit in the account.

Solution

Here P = K250 000
r = 0.08

n = 4 years
S = ?

Using $S = P (1 + r)^n$

$= K250\ 000 (1 + 0.08)^4$

$= K250\ 000 (0.08)^4$

$= K250\ 000 \times 1.36048896$

$= K340\ 122.\ 24$ as given in example 17

Total interest earned $= P (1 + r) n - P$

$= K340\ 122.24 - K250\ 000$

$= K90\ 122.24$ again as calculated in example 17

CALCULATING COMPOUND INTEREST: FUTURE VALUE

Example 19

Find the compound interest on K100 000 at 10% per annum for 4 years.

Solution

Given P = K100 000
r = 0.1
n = 4 years
S =?

Using $S = P (1 + r)^n$

$= K100\ 000 (1 + 0.1)^4$

$= K100\ 000 (1.1)^4$

$= K100\ 000 \times 1.4641$

$= \underline{K146\ 410}$

CALCULATING THE COMPOUND INTEREST RATE

Example 20

At what rate of compound interest should K100 000 deposited now in a savings account for 4 years take to become K146 410?

Solution

Here P = K100 000
S = K146 410

$$n = 4 \text{ years}$$
$$r = ?$$

Using $S = P(1 + r)^n$

$$K146\ 410 = K100\ 000\ (1 + r)^4$$

Dividing by K100 000 on both sides

$$1.4641 = (1 + r)^4$$

Taking the 4th root on both sides

$$\sqrt[4]{1.4641} = 1 + r$$

$$1.1 = 1 + r$$

Making r the subject of the formula

$$r = 1.1 - 1$$

$$= 0.1$$

Thus, r = <u>10%</u>

CALCULATING THE NUMBER YEARS

Example 21

How long will K100 000 invested today in a savings account giving 10% compound interest rate take to become K146 410?

Solution

Here P = K100 000
  S = K146 410
  n = ?
  r = 0.1

Using $S = P(1 + r)^n$

$$K146\ 410 = K100\ 000\ (1 + 0.1)^n$$

$$K146\ 410 = K100\ 000\ (1.1)^n$$

Dividing by K100 000 on both sides

1.46 410 = $(1.1)^n$

To solve for n in the above equation, we employ the logarithm as follows:

Log 1.46410 = n log 1.1

$n = \dfrac{\log 1.46410}{\log 1.1} = \dfrac{0.16557074}{0.041392685}$

Thus, n = 4 years

CALCULATING THE AMOUNT TO BE INVESTED

Example 22

An investor wants to have K146 410 after 4 years by depositing a certain amount in a savings account giving 10% compound interest per annum. How much should he invest now?

Solution

Here S = K146 410
     P =?
     r = 0.1
     n = 4 years

Using $S = P(1 + r)^n$

K146 410 = $P(1 +0.1)^4$

K146 410 = $P(1.1)^4$

K146 410 = P (1.4641)

P = $\dfrac{K146\ 410}{1.4641}$

  = K100 000

Thus, the investor needs to deposit K100 000 now to have K146 410 after 4 years, if the account gives 10% compound interest

Have you noticed that examples 19 through to 22 contain the same information? All i did was to change figures so that in example 19 we calculated S, example 20 -r, example 21 -n and example 22 -P. Thus, it is the same formula $S = P(1 + r)^n$ that has been used throughout!

DIFFERENT TYPES OF INVESTMENT PROBLEMS

Investment problems may take any of the following forms:

1. If you invest Kx now for n time period at an interest rate of r per time period, how much will your investment be worth at the end of time period?

2. If you want to have a fixed sum of money Kx at the end of n time period, how much would you need to invest now at an interest rate r per time period in order to have Kx at the end of that time?

3. If you invest Kx each time period for n time period earning interest rate at r per time period, what will be the value of your investment at the end of that period? Example if you invest K100 a month in a savings that pays interest at 0.25%. What will your investment be worth at the end of 5 years, that is, 60 time periods?

COMPOUNDING AND INFLATION

The same compounding formula could be used to predict future prices after allowing inflation. All that is required is to substitute interest rate r for inflation rate r.

Hence the formula is

$$S = P (1 + r)^n$$

Where S = future value
P = present value
r = inflation rate
n = number of years

Example 23

What will be the salary of a Bank Clerk in five years' time given that she earns K800 000 and wage inflation is expected to be 10% per annum?

Solution

Here S = ?
P = K800 000
n = 5 years
r = 0.1

$S = K800\ 000(1+0.1)^5$

= <u>K1, 288,408</u>

She is expected to earn K1, 288,408.

SPECIAL DETOURS IN COMPOUNDING

In this section we take a look at the practical aspect of compounding. In reality, interest rates are likely to change over time, amount invested may be increased or reduced, compounding may be for a period less than one year or indeed a combination of years and months. All these circumstances bring about deviations from the norm of compounding.

CHANGES IN INTEREST RATES

If interest rates change over a period of time, the terminal value can be calculated using the following formula:

$$S = P(1 + r) \times (1 + r_2)^{n-x}$$

Where S =?
P = present value
r_1 = initial interest rate
r_2 = next interest rate
n – x = number of years in which interest rate r_2 applies.
x = number of years in which interest rate r_1 applies

Example 24

If K20 000 000 is invested now to earn 10% per annum for 3 years and then 8% per annum in the two subsequent years, what would be the size of the total investment at the end of five years?

Solution

Here P = K20 000 000
$r^1 = 0.1$
$r^2 = 0.08$
x = 3 years
n = 5 years
S = ?

Using $S = P(1 + r1)^x (1 + 0.1)^{n-x}$

$= K20\ 000\ 000 (1 + 0.1)^3 (1 + 0.08)^{5-3}$

$= K20\ 000\ 000 (1.1)^3 (1.08)^2$

$= K20\ 000\ 000 \times 1.331 \times 1.1664$

$= \underline{K31, 049,568}$

Note: In the example above interest rates have fallen from 10% to 8% over a period of 5 years. The same principles are applied when interest rates increase.

INCREASING THE SUM INVESTED

If the amount invested over time increases, the terminal value can be calculated using the following formula:

$$S = P(1 + r)^n + \left[\frac{a(1 + r)^n - a}{r}\right]$$

Where P = present value or initial investment
a = further amount invested
n = the year to which the investment is valued
r = interest rate

Example 25

Suppose a person invests K400 000 now and a further K300 000 each year for 4 years, how much would the total investment be worth after 4 years if interest is earned at a rate of 10% per annum?

Solution

Here P = K400 000
a = K300 000
r = 0.1
n = 4 years

Using $S = P(1 + r)^n + \left[\frac{a(1 + r)^n - a}{r}\right]$

$= K400\ 000\ (1 + 0.1)^4 + \frac{K300\ 000\ (1 + 0.1)^4 - K300\ 000}{0.1}$

$= K400\ 000\ (1.1)^4 + \frac{K300\ 000\ (1.1)^4 - K300\ 000}{0.1}$

$= K585\ 640 + \frac{K439\ 230 - K300\ 000}{0.1}$

$= K585\ 640 + K1392\ 300$

$= \underline{K1,\ 977,940}$

Note that the above formula can be used to calculate the amount left on deposit if a person withdraws fixed amounts from the bank each year.
Check example 22.

Example 26

Suppose a person deposits K20 000 000 at the beginning of the year at 5% per annum compound. He withdraws K2000 000 at the end of each year. What would be the sum available after 4 years?

Solution

Here P = K20 000 000
a = -K200 000 (negative because he withdraws)
r = 0.05
n = 4 years
S = ?

Using $S = P(1 + r)^n + \dfrac{a(1 + r)^n - a}{r}$

$= K20\ 000\ 000\ (1 + 0.05)^4 + \dfrac{-K2000\ 000\ (1 + 0.05)^4 - (-K2000\ 000)}{0.05}$

$= K20\ 000\ 000\ (1.05)^4 + \dfrac{-K2000\ 000\ (1.05)^4 - (-K2000\ 000)}{0.05}$

$= K24\ 310\ 125 - \dfrac{K2,431,012.5 + K2000\ 000}{0.05}$

$= K24, 310, 125 - K8, 620, 250$

= K15, 689, 875

MORE FREQUENT COMPOUNDING: NOMINAL AND EFFECTIVE RATES

Even though interest rates are usually quoted on an annual basis, most interest is compounded quarterly, semi-annually, monthly, weekly or daily. Thus, if we are told that a bank pays 6% interest on savings accounts compounded quarterly, this does not mean that it actually pays 6% every 3 months or that it actually pays 6% a year, but that it pays a fourth of 6% or 1.5% every 3 months. Similarly, if a mortgage company charge 9% compounded monthly, this means that it charges a twelfth of 9%, namely ¾ of 1% each month.

In compounding, the time interval between successive calculations and additions of the interest is called the **conversion period**, for example if the conversion period is 6 months, we say that interest is compounded semi-annually. Similarly, the interest rate applicable in a particular period is called the **periodic rate**.

It cannot be emphasized how important it is for us to use the correct number of conversion periods and periodic rate in our calculations. These are determined using the following equations:

Periodic rate = $\dfrac{\text{annual interest rate}}{\text{Conversion period}}$

For example, 6% compounded quarterly gives:

Periodic rate = $\dfrac{\text{annual interest rate}}{\text{Conversion rate}}$ = $\dfrac{6\%}{4}$ = 1.5%

> Number of conversion period = number of years X conversion period

For 6% compounded quarterly for 6 years gives the total number of conversion periods 6 X 4 = 24 periods.

RULES APPLIED IN CALCULATING COMPOUND AMOUNT

The following rules must be learnt by heart.

1. If compounding is being done semi-annually, divide r by 2 and multiply n by 2.
2. If compounding is being done quarterly, divide r by 4 and multiply n by 4.
3. If compounding is being done monthly, divide r by 12 and multiply n by 12.
4. If compounding is being done weekly, divide r by 52 and multiply n by 52.
5. If compounding is being done daily, divide r by 365 and multiply n by 365.

COMPOUND AMOUNT UNDER MORE FREQUENT COMPOUNDING

The formula which we can use to calculate the compound amount under more frequent compounding is

$$A = P\left(1 + \frac{r}{m}\right)^{nm}$$

Where n = now the total number of conversion periods rather than the number of years
r = nominal interest per year
m = conversion period
A = compound amount

Example 27

If we invest K5000 000 at 8% compounded quarterly, after 3years, find the total investment after 3 years.

Solution

Here P = K5000 000
r = 0.08
m = 4
nm = 4 X 3 = 12 periods
A = ?

Using $A = P\left(1 + \frac{r}{m}\right)^{nm}$

$$= K5000\ 000 \left(1 + \frac{0.08}{4}\right)^{12}$$

$$= K5000\ 000\ (1 + 0.02)^{12}$$

$$= K5000\ 000\ (1.02)^{12}$$

$$= K5000\ 000 \times 1.268241795$$

$$= \underline{K6,\ 341,208.97}$$

NOMINAL AND EFFECTIVE RATES

As I pointed out above, if money is invested at 6% compounded quarterly, this does not mean that it will actually yield 6%. This is only what is called **nominal interest rate**, and to determine the actual rate or the **effective rate**, we use the following formula:

$$j = \left(1 + \frac{r}{m}\right)^{m} - 1$$

Where j = effective annual rate
　　　r = nominal interest rate
　　　m = number of conversion periods in a year

Example 28

Find the effective rate for an investment which pays 8%

　　a)　compounded semi-annually
　　b)　compounded quarterly
　　c)　compounded monthly
　　d)　compounded weekly
　　e)　compounded daily

Solution

Using $j = \left(1 + \frac{r}{m}\right)^{m} - 1$ in all cases, we have.

a) $j = \left(1 + \frac{0.08}{2}\right)^{2} - 1$

　　$= (1 + 0.04)^{2} - 1$

　　$= (1.04)^{2} - 1$

　　$= 1.0816 - 1$

$= 0.081$

$= \underline{8.16\%}$

b) $j = \left(1 + \dfrac{0.08}{4}\right)^{4} - 1$

$= (1 + 0.02)^{4} - 1$

$= (1.02)^{4} - 1$

$= 1.08243216 - 1$

$= 0.08243216$

$= \underline{8.24\%}$

c) $j = \left(1 + \dfrac{0.08}{12}\right)^{12} - 1$

$= (1 + 0.006666667)^{12} - 1$

$= (1.06666667)^{12} - 1$

$= 1.082999507 - 1$

$= 0.082999507$

$= \underline{8.30\%}$

d) $j = \left(1 + \dfrac{0.08}{52}\right)^{52} - 1$

$= (1 + 0.01538462)^{52} -$

$= (1.001538462)^{52} - 1$

$= 0.083220474$

$= \underline{8.32\%}$

e) $j = \left(1 + \dfrac{0.08}{365}\right)^{365} - 1$

$= (1 + 0.000219178)^{365} - 1$

$= (1.000219178)^{365} - 1$

$= 1.083277571 - 1$

= 0.08327757

= 8.33%

EQUIVALENT RATES

Two annual rates of interest with different conversion periods are called **equivalent** if they yield the same compound amount at the end of one year. Check example below.

Example 29

Find the compound amount of K1000 000 at the end of one year at:

a) 4% compounded quarterly
b) 4.06% compounded annually

Solution

Using $A = P\left[1 + \dfrac{r}{m}\right]^{nm}$

For (a) P = K1000 000
    r = 4
    m = 4
    n = 1
    A = ?

$= K1000\ 000\left[1 + \dfrac{0.04}{4}\right](1)^4$

$= K1000\ 0000\ (1.1)^4$

$= K1000\ 000 \times 1.04060401$

$= K1,\ 040604.01$

For (b) P = K1000 000
    r = 4.06
    m = 1
    n = 1
    A = ?

$A = K1000\ 000\left[1 + \dfrac{0.0406}{1}\right]^1$

$= K1000\ 000\ (1.0406)$

$= K1,\ 040,600$

Since the two amounts are similar when rounded off to nearest hundreds, 4% compounded quarterly and 4.06% compounded annually are said to be equivalent rates.

Example 31

Find the effective rate r equivalent to the nominal rate 9% compounded monthly.

Solution

Taking one year, K1 effective rate will amount to $1 + r$.

Thus, $1 + r = \left[1 + \dfrac{r}{m} \right]^n$

$= 1 + r = \left[1 + \dfrac{0.09}{12} \right]^{12}$

$= 1 + r = (1 + 0.0075)^{12}$

$= 1 + r = (1.0075)^{12}$

$= 1 + r = 1.093806898$

$= r = 1.093806898 - 1$

$= 0.093806898$

$= \underline{9.38\%}$

Example 32

Find the nominal rate j compounded quarterly which is equivalent to 9% effective.

Solution

In one year K1 at j compounded quarterly will amount to $\left(1 + \dfrac{j}{4} \right)^4$

And 9% effective will amount to $(1 + 0.09)^1$

Thus, from above, we can equate the two quantities as follows and then solve for j.

$\left(1 + \dfrac{j}{4} \right)^4 = (1 + 0.09)^1$

$\left(1 + \dfrac{j}{4} \right)^4 = 1.09$

Taking the fourth root on both sides gives

$$= 1 + \frac{j}{4} = \sqrt[4]{1.09}$$

$$= 1 + \frac{j}{4} = 1.021778181$$

$$= \frac{j}{4} = 1.021778181 - 1$$

$$j = 0.087112724$$

$$= \underline{8.71\%}$$

Example 33

Two local banks in Lusaka Bank A and Bank B both charge 9% interest on advances but compounded differently. For Bank A interest is compounded quarterly but for Bank B it is compounded semi-annually. As a financial adviser, which bank would you recommend your customer?

Solution

The best source of advance will be from the bank that charges lower actual interest rate. Hence to determine which is which we need to determine the effective rate for each bank.

Effective rate, j is calculated using the following formula

$$j = \left(1 + \frac{r}{m}\right)^m - 1$$

For Bank A, $j = \left(1 + \frac{0.09}{4}\right)^4 - 1$

$$= (1 + 0.0225)^4 - 1$$

$$= (1.0225)^4 - 1$$

$$= 1.093083319$$

$$= 0.093083319$$

$$= \underline{9.31\%}$$

For Bank B, $j = \left(1 + \frac{0.09}{2}\right)^2 - 1$

$$= (1 + 0.045)^2 - 1$$

$$= (1.045)^2 - 1$$

$$= 1.092025 - 1$$

$$= 0.092025$$

$$= \underline{9.20\%}$$

Bank B charges lower actual rate of 9.29% compared to Bank A's is cheaper for this customer to get an advance from Bank B (holding other things constant).

AN ADDENDUM

Some compounding computations may involve both years and months. If this is the case, how do we then compute the maturity value or future value?

Well, the usual approach is to compound the years as usual but multiply the answer by the figure involving month's component. The example below illustrates the technique.

Example 34

Find the compound amount of K10 000 000 for 9 years 4 months at 8%.

Solution

Here P = K10 000 000
     n = 9 years
     r = 0.08

Using $\boxed{S = P\,(1 + r)^n\,(1 + rn)}$

Where P = present value
     S = future value
     n = number of interest periods
     r = interest rate

Thus, $S = K10\,000\,000\,(1 + 0.08)^9\left(1 + 0.08 \times \dfrac{4}{12}\right)$

$= K10\,000\,000\,(1.08)^9\,(1 + 0.08 \times \tfrac{1}{3})$

$= K10\,000\,000 \times 1.999004627 \times 1.026666666$

$= \underline{K20,523,114.16}$

Note that the above is made up of compound interest for 9 interest periods or years and simple interest on the compound amount for 4 months or $\frac{1}{3}$ year. The same principles are followed when the problem involves determining the present value but where n is given in years and months.

DEPRECIATION

Depreciation is defined as the loss of value of non-current assets due to tear and wear, which in turn is caused by usage, affluxion of time, obsolescence or depletion.

There are many methods that a company can employ to depreciate its non current assets. The two most common methods are:

4. *Straight-line method* – this is where the same depreciable amount is allocated each year calculated on the basis of cost.

- To use the straight-line method, we need information on the following aspects:

   a) Cost of the non current asset
   b) Estimated useful life in years of the non current asset
   c) Estimated scrap or residue value of the non current asset.

Depreciation charge can then be determined using the following formula

> Depreciation charge = $\dfrac{\text{Cost – scrap value}}{\text{Estimated useful life in years}}$

Example 35

Find the depreciation charge for a company's non current asset which cost K12 000 0000, and has no residue value after 5 years.

Solution

Here cost = K12 000 000
Scrap value = K0
Useful life = 5 years

Using Depreciation Charge = $\dfrac{\text{Cost – Scrap value}}{\text{Useful life in years}}$

$$= \frac{\text{K12 000 000} - 0}{5}$$

$$= \frac{\text{K12 000 000}}{5}$$

$$= \underline{\text{K2 400 000}} \text{ per annum would be the}$$
depreciation charge

5. Compound depreciation – this is also called the *reducing balance method.* It is a method where the depreciable amount keeps on changing every year and is calculated on the written down value or the Net Book Value (NBV) of the non current asset.

   Compound depreciation is similar to compound interest except that instead of adding interest, we subtract depreciation. This means that the present value of the non current asset will be greater than the future value of that asset.

The following formula is used:

$$B = D (1 - r)^n$$

Where B = B00k value or present value of the non current asset
        D = cost of the non current asset
        r = depreciation rate expressed as a proportion
        n = useful life of the asset in years

The above formula can be used to find either B, r, or D as the following examples illustrate.

Example 36

A new machine costing K8 000 000 has a useful life of 10 years after which it can be sold for K100 000. Calculate the annual rate of compound depreciation.

Solution

Here D = K8 000 000
      B = K100 000
      n = 10 years
      r =?

Using $B = D (1 - r)^n$

K100 000 = K 8 000 000 $(1 - r)^{10}$

 Dividing by K8 000 000 on both sides

= 0.0125 = $(1 - r)^{10}$

Taking the tenth root on both sides

$$= \sqrt[10]{0.0125} = 1 - r$$

= 0.645195012 = 1 - r

r = 1 - 0.645195012

r = 0.354804988 = <u>35.48%</u>

Example 37

A new machine cost K8 000 000 and is depreciated at 35.48% per annum. What is the book value of the new machine when it is 10 years old?

Solution

Here D = K8 000 000
    B =?
    n = 10 years
    r = 35.48%

Using $B = D (1 - r)^n$

    $= K8\ 000\ 000\ (1 - 0.3548)^{10}$

    $= K8\ 000\ 000\ (0.6452)^{10}$

    $= K8\ 000\ 000 \times 0.012500966$

    <u>= K100 0007.728</u>

Which is K100 000 when rounded off correct to hundreds.

Example 38

A new machine cost K 8000 000 and is depreciated at 35.48% per annum. After how many years will its book value closer to K100 000?

Solution

Here D = K8 000 000
    B = K100 000
    r = 35.48%
    n =?

Using $B = D (1 - r)^n$

$K100\ 000 = K8\ 000\ 000\ (1 - 03548)^n$

Dividing by K8000 000 on both sides

$0.0125 = (0.6452)^n$

To solve for n we introduce logarithms as follows:

$\text{Log } 0.0125 = n \log 0.6452$

$n = \dfrac{\log 0.0125}{\log 0.6452}$

$= \dfrac{^{-}1.903089987}{^{-}0.190305641}$

$= 10.00017644$

<u>= 10 years</u>

Again that was the same question only requiring the change in the subject of the formula for compound depreciation.

DISCOUNTING

Discounting is the reverse of compounding. Its major application in business is in the evaluation of capital expenditure projects to decide whether they offer a satisfactory return to the investor. This technique is called the *Discounting Cash flow* (DCF). DCF involves calculating the present value of

the future value discounted at a given discount rate for a given number of years.

Just like interest calculations, discounting calculations may also be divided However, in contract to simple interest problems, where the interest rate applies to the principal amount P (to which it is added at the end of each year), in simple discount problems the rate is applied to the amount A due at the end n years (from which it is subtracted fro each year).

SIMPLE DISCOUNT AT A DISCOUNT RATE

The simple discount at a discount rate otherwise called the bank discount is given by the following formula

$$D = Adn$$

Where D = simple discount
  A = principal amount or sum
  d = discount rate
  n = number of years

Meanwhile, if the discount rate is **d**, the **present value** is given by the formula.

$$P = A (1 - dn)$$

Where p = present value
  A = future value
  d = discount rate
  n = number of years

Example 39

Find the present value of K4000 000 due at the end of three years if the discount rate is 9.5%

Solution

Here A = K4000 0000
  d = 9.5% = 0.095

n = 3
P = ?

Using P = A (1 – dn)

$= K4000\ 000\ (1 - 0.095\ X\ 3)$

$= K4000\ 000\ (1 - 0.285$

$= K4000\ 0000\ (0.75)$

$= K2860\ 000$

Note the order of operation when using the simple discount at a discount rate formula. We multiply d and n before subtracting from 1. Thus, the present value of K4000 000 discounted for 3 years at 9.5% is K2,860,000.

Example 40

Find the simple discount of a debt of K5 000 000 due in 7 months a discount rate of 5%. Also find the present value of the debt.

Solution

Here A = K45 000 000
d = 0.05
$n = \dfrac{7}{12}$
D =?

Using D = Adn
$= K45\ 000\ 000\ X\ 0.05\ X\ \dfrac{7}{12}$

$= \underline{K1,\ 312,499.97}$

P = A (1 – dn)

$= K45\ 000\ 000 \left(1 - 0.05\ X\ \dfrac{7}{12}\right)$

$= K45\ 000\ 000\ (1 - 0.29166666)$

$= K45\ 000\ 000\ (0.970833334$

$= \underline{K43,\ 687,500.03}$

SIMPLE DISCOUNT AT AN INTEREST RARE

Note that the bank discount is also called *interest in advance*.

Simple discount may also be determined at an interest rate though this is rarely used in practice as it complicates calculations.

The discount value of A at an interest rate is given by:

$$D = A - P$$

Where D = simple discount at an interest rate
      A = Amount or future value
      P = present value

The present value is then given as:

$$P = \frac{A}{1 + rn}$$

Where P = present value
      A = Amount or future value
      r = interest rate
      n = number of years.

Example 41

Find the present value on K45 000 000 at 5% simple interest due in 7 months. Also find the time discount.

Solution

Here A = K45 000 000
      r = 0.05
      $n = \frac{7}{12}$
      P = ?

Using $P = \frac{A}{1 + rn}$

$$= \frac{K45\ 000\ 000}{1 + \left(0.05 \times \frac{7}{12}\right)}$$

$$= \frac{K45\ 000\ 000}{1.029166666}$$

$$= \underline{K43\ 724\ 696.38}$$

The true discount is given by:

$$D = A - P$$

$$= K45\ 000\ 000 - K43\ 724\ 696.38\ =\ \underline{K1275\ 303.62}$$

COMPOUND DISCOUNT

As alluded to earlier compound discount is the reverse of compound interest. We use the same compound interest formula but instead make P the subject of the formula. In discounting we find the present value of a given future value.

The compound discount formula is given below.

$$P = \frac{A}{(1 + r)^n} \text{ or } P = A(1 + r)^{-n}$$

Where = P = present value

A = future value or sum
r = discount rate
n = number of years

In the above formula, the quantity $(1 + r)^{-n}$ is called the discount factor. The value can be got directly from compound discount tables, but it has to be computed using a calculator. Again if we are using a calculator for it is advisable that we use all the digits from the calculator and only round off our final result.

Example 42

Find the discount factors for the following to 4 decimal places.

a) n = 10, r = 15%
b) n = 3, r = 5%
c) for 9 years at 3 % compound interest

Solution

Using $(1 + r)^n$

a) $(1 + 0.15)^{-10} = (1.15)^{-10} = 0.247184706 = 0.2472$

b) $(1 + 0.15)^{-3} = (1.05)^{-3} = 0.863837598 = 0.8638$

c) $(1 + 0.03)^{-9} = (1.03)^{-9} = 0766416732 = 0.7664$

Example 43

A man wants to know the sum he has to invest at 8% compounded annually to have K20 000 000 available in 18 years for the higher education of a child. How much should he invest now?

Solution

Here A = K20 000 000

r = 0.08
n = 18
P = ?

Using P = A $(1 + r)^{-n}$

= K20 000 000 $(1 + 0.08)^{-18}$

= K20 000 000 $(1.08)^{-18}$

= K20 000 000 X 0.25029029

= <u>K5, 004,980.58</u>

Thus, the man should invest K5,004,980.58 now to have K20 000 000 after 18 years at 8% compound interest.

If compounding is done any other the following formula should be used instead:

$$P = \left(1 + \frac{r}{m}\right)^{-n}$$

Where A = future value
       n = number of conversion periods
       r = interest rate
       m = conversion frequency

The compound discount formula enables us to determine how much money we must invest to receive a fixed amount n years hence, how much will get now for a note to which we agree to pay a fixed amount n years hence, how much we should have invested a number of years ago to meet certain obligations due now, etc.

Example 44

Find how much money I should have invested 10 years ago at 4% compounded quarterly to have a current balance of K12 000 000.

Solution

Here A = K12 000 000
       r = $\frac{4\%}{4}$ = 1% = 0.01
       m = 4
       n = 10 X4 = 40
       P = ?

Using P = A $\left(1 + \frac{r}{m}\right)^{-n}$

$$= \text{K12 0000 000} \left(1 + \frac{0.04}{4} \right)^{-40}$$

$$= \text{K12 000 000} (1.01)^{-40}$$

$$= \text{K12 000 000} (0.671653138)$$
$$= \text{K8, 059,837.656}$$

$$= \underline{\text{K8, 059,837.66}}$$

PROGRESS CLINIC 6

1. A sum of money is deposited now at 10% per annum. How long will it take to double?

2. K1000 000 is invested now, and the investor is prepared to leave it on deposit for 15 years. What rate of interest would it be necessary to earn if the sum invested is to grow to K7 500 000.

3. complete the table below

	Years required for investment to		
	Double	Treble	Quadruple
Compound rate 8% 12% 16% 20%			

4. Estimate the market price of a holding of 7% Treasury bill with a nominal value of k125 000 000 and 4 years to run maturity, If the current rate of interest is 10%

5. If K9 500 is invested on the first January of a certain year of 12% compounded and K800 000 is withdrawn at the end of each year. How much would remain after 12 years.

6. A machine costing K12 500 000 now need replacing in 6 year's time

a. Estimate its replacement price if the rate of inflation is 11% per annum.
b. How much must be set aside.

(i)   at the beginning of each year

(ii)   at the end of each year

7. A man borrows a sum of money for which he is charged 8.5% simple interest. How much did he borrow originally, if he owes K9 700 000 after 2.5 years.

8. A manufacturer bought K160 000 worth of new tools in 1999. If these tools are being depreciated linearly over a period of 8 years, what is their value?

a. in 60 days

b. in 120 days

9. Mr. Motorist wants to borrow K400 000 to buy a second hand Toyota Dx and pay off the loan with monthly payments stretched over a period of 3 years. If the dealer charges him 9% interest and computes the month due in 3 years by dividing the total amount due in 3 years by 36, how much will Mr. Motorists have to pay each month?

a) 5% compounded quarterly

b) 8% compounded semi-annually

c) 9% compounded monthly

10.   If K1 200 is borrowed at 8% compounded quarterly and K1000 000 is repaid after 2 years, how much is still owed at that time?

11.   If K6000 000 is invested at 6%, what is the value of each investment after 4 years if:

a) interest is compounded annually

b) interest is compounded semi-annually

c) interest is compounded quarterly

d) interest is compounded monthly

12.   A college needs K2000 000 000 two years from now to built its own campus. What sum should be set aside now and invested at 8% compounded quarterly so that the K2000 000 000 will be available when needed?

13.   To clear up a debt, Mr. Borrower agrees to pay K1000 000 now, another K1000 000 a year from now and another K1000 000 two years from now. If the future payments are discounted at 9% compounded monthly, what is the present value of these three payments?

14.   A firm will have to spend K300 000 000 on new plant in two years now. Currently investment rates are at a nominal 10%.

a) What single sum should now be invested, if compounding is semi-annually?

b) What is the effective rate?

15.   A mainframe computer whose cost is k22 000 000 will depreciate to a scrap value of K12 000 000 in 5 years.

a) If the reducing balance method of depreciation is used, find the depreciation rate.

b) What is the book value of the computer at the end of the third year.

c) How much more e book value be at the end of the third year if the straight-line method of depreciation had been used?

    a. Find the present value of a debt of K2 500 000 taken out for 4 years (with no intermediate repayment) where borrowing rate is 12%.

CHAPTER 7

CAPITAL INVESTMENT APPRAISAL

INTRODUCTION

The DCF (Discounted Cash Flow) involves the application of discounting arithmetic to the estimated future cash flows from a project in order to decide whether a project is expected to earn a satisfactory rate of return.

DCF can be used either for a single project which has to be undertaken or assessing a number of projects for which only one should be undertaken if the results are satisfactory. It is important to note that in investment appraisal projects are assumed to be mutually exclusive i.e. only one project can be undertaken mainly due to scarcity of resources. Therefore, the key question is always 'which one of these projects should the firm invest in?'

There are two methods, namely Net Present Value (NPV) and Internal Rate of Return (IRR). It is important to note that it is the cash flow of project that are discounted not the profits.

NET PRESENT VALUE

This is the difference between the present value of cash – inflows and present value of cash flows.

NPV = PV of cash inflows – PV of cash outflows

NPV CALCULATION FOR SINGLE CASH FLOW PROJECTS

These are projects with only one cash inflow and one cash outflow. The NPV for such projects is simply the difference between present value of future receipt and the cost as given below:

NPV = F$(1+r)^{-n}$ –Cost

Where F = Future receipt
  r = discount rate
  n = number of years

Example 1

A firm needs to choose between two projects, projects A and B. Project A requires an initial outlay of k200 million and yields k227million in two years' time. Project B requires an initial outlay of k173 million and yields k200 million kwacha after two years. Which of these projects would you advise the firm to invest in if the annual market rate of interest is 5%?.

Solution

$NPV = F(1+r)^{-n} - Cost$

Project A; $NPV = 227\ 000\ 000(1.05)^{-2} - 200\ 000\ 000 = k\ 5,895,691.61$

Project B; $NPV = 200\ 000\ 000(1.05)^{-2} - 173\ 000\ 000 = k\ 8,405,895.69$

Though both projects are worthwhile for investment purposes, project B is preferred as it gives a higher positive NPV compared to project A.

NPV CALCULATION FOR MULTIPLE CASH FLOW PROJECTS

When performing NPV calculations for multiple cash flow projects, the following approach should be taken.

a) Identify the relevant cash flows and out flows of a project not forgetting the initial investment.

b) Set up a table and discount each of the cash flow to its present value using the companies required rate of return.

c) Calculate the net present value of the project by taking the out flows away from the inflows.

d) Decide whether or not the project should be accepted.

e) The initial investment period is always taken to be year zero and has a discount factor of 1.000.

f) Figures in brackets in the table indicate negatives that is cash out flows

Year	Discount factor	Cash flow (k)	Present value (k)
0	1.000	( )	( )
		NPV =	

- Present value = Discount factor x cash flow
- NPV = present value of inflows – present value of outflows.
- Discount factor is calculated using $(1 + r)-n$, where r is the discount rate and n is the number of years.

DECISION CRITERIA

To decide whether or not the project should be taken the following rules apply:

1) If the project has a positive NPV then accept the project i.e.
   NPV > 0

2) If the project has NPV equal to zero, then the project breaks even i.e.
   NPV = 0

3) If a project has a negative NPV then it is rejected i.e. NPV < 0

4) If more than one project is being accessed, the one with the highest NPV is preferred.

ADVANTAGES OF NPV

1) Shareholder wealth is maximized
2) It takes into account the time value of money
3) It is based on cash flows which are less subjective than profits

DISADVANTAGES OF NPV

1) Difficult to identify an appropriate discount rate
2) Cash flows are assumed to occur at the end of the year, but in practice, this is over simplistic
3) Some manager are unfamiliar with the concept of NPV
4) The cash flows are estimates with a lot of errors arising as a result of changes in operating environment.

INTERVAL RATE RETURN (IRR)

This is the discount rate at which the net present value of a project is exactly equal to zero.

CALCULATING IRR FOR SINGLE CASH FOW PROJECTS

The following formula is used:

$$NPV = \text{initial cost} + \frac{\text{Future cash flows}}{(1+IRR)^n}$$

Where IRR = discount rate

Since IRR is defined as the discount rate where the NPV of a project = 0; then the left hand side of the above equation = 0. Then we substitute the values for initial cost and future cash flows together with n and then solve for IRR as illustrated below.

Example 2

A firm can make investment of k1.7 billion now and receive k2 billion in 2 years time. What is the IRR?

Solution

$$0 = -1.7 + \frac{2}{(1+IRR)^2}$$

$$1.7 = \frac{2}{(1+IRR)^2}$$

$1.7(1+IRR)^2 = 2$

Dividing both sides by 1.7 we have;

$(1+IRR)^2 = 1.176470588$

Taking the squre root on both sides, we have;

$1+IRR = 1.084652289$

$IRR = 1.084652289 - 1$

$= 0.84652289$

$= 8.465\%$

IRR CALCULATION FOR MULTIPLE CASH FLOW PROJECTS

The following are the four steps to an IRR calculation:

1) Calculate the project NPV at any reasonable discount rate if this is not given in an exam

2) If the above NPV is positive, choose a higher discount rate a, calculate the NPV again if the above NPV was negative, choose a lower discount rate.

3) Either way, you must end p with one positive and one negative NPV. The IRR now be calculated using the following interpolation formula:

$$IRR = (A\% + \underline{a} \quad X (B - A) \%)$$
$$a - b$$

Where
A = lower discount rate
B = higher discount rate
a = NPV at lower rate
b = NPV at higher rate

4) The IRR must be compared to the companies required rate of return to decide whether or not the project should be accepted.

DECISION CRITERIA

a) If IRR is greater than the companies required rate of return, then the project is accepted.

b) If IRR is less than the company's required rate of return, the project is rejected

c) If more than one project is being assessed, the one with the highest IRR is preferred

ADVANTAGES OF IRR

1) It takes into account the time value of money

2) Results are expressed as a simple percentage and more easily understood than other methods.

3) It indicates now sensitive decisions are to a change in interest rate

DISADVANTAGES

a) project with unconventional cash flows, can have either negative or multiple IRR which are confusing to the user

b) IRR can be confused with ARR or ROCE since all methods give answers in percentage terms. Hence a cash based method can be confused with a profit based method.

c) It may give conflicting recommendations to NPV.

d) Some managers are unfamiliar with IRR method.

e) It cannot accommodate changes in rate over the life of a project

f) It fails to distinguish two projects with similar IRR

g) It assumes funds are reinvested at a rate equivalent to the IRR itself which may be realistically high.

Example 3

An initial investment of K75 000 000 in a business guarantees the following cash flows:

Year	Cash flow
3	K24 000 000
4	K30 000 000
5	K42 000 000

Assume an interest rate of 4.5% compounded semi-annually

a) Find the NPV of the cash flows

b)   Is the investment profitable

Solution

a) Since compounding is done semi-annually, we multiply the years by 2 and divide the interest rate by 2. Hence r = 0.0225, n = 6, 8, 10.

Year (periods)	Discount Factor at 2.25%	Cash flow	Present value
0	1.000	(75 000 000)	(75 000 000)
6	0.875	24 000 000	21 000 000
8	0.837	30 000 000	25 110 000
10	0.801	42 000 000	33 642 000
			4 752 000

b) The investment is profitable as it has a positive NPV. NPV is superior to IRR for various reasons and should therefore prevail over IRR whenever the two give conflicting recommendations.

Example 4

A firm is consider two separate mutually exclusive capital projects with cash flows as follows.

Year	0	1	2	3	4	5
Project A	(80 000)	18 000	20 000	25 000	38 000	45 000
Project B	(120 000)	30 000	50 000	50 000	50 000	15 000

a) Using the NPV criterion and a discount rate of 15%, choose the project that is more profitable

b) Find the NPV using a discount rate of 20% and use the results to estimate the IRR for each project.

c) verify that, using the IRR criterion, the decision in (a) is reserved and attempt to explain why

Solution

a) NPV computation at 15%

Year	DF at 15%	Project A Cash flow	PV	Project B Cash flow	PV
0	1.000	(80 000)	(80 000)	(120 000)	(120 000)
1	0.870	18 000	15 660	30 000	26 000
2	0.756	20 000	15 120	50 000	37 800
3	0.658	25 000	16 450	50 000	32 900
4	0.572	38 000	21 736	50 000	28 600
5	0.497	45 000	22 365	15 000	7 455
		NPV	11 331		12 855

From above both projects are profitable but project B is more profitable hence the best choice.

b) NPV Computation at 20%

Year	DF at 20%	Project A Cash flow	PV	Project B Cash flow	PV
0	1.000	(80 000)	(80 000)	(120 000)	(120 000)
1	0.833	18 000	14 994	30 000	24 990
2	0.694	20 000	13 880	50 000	34 700
3	0.579	25 000	14 475	50 000	28 950
4	0.482	38 000	18 316	50 000	24 100
5	0.402	45 000	18 090	15 000	6 030
		NPV	(245)		(1 230)

$$IRR = A\% + \left[\frac{a}{a-b} \ (B-A)\% \right]$$

Project A: $15\% + \left[\frac{11331}{11331 - (-245)} (20-15)\% \right]$

$$15\% + \left[\frac{11331}{11576} \ X \ 5 \right]$$

$$= \underline{19.89\%}$$

Positive B: $\left[15\% + \frac{12855}{12\ 855 - (1230)} \ (20-15)\% \right]$

$$15\% + \left[\frac{12855}{14085} \ X \ 5 \right]$$

$$= \underline{19.56\%}$$

c) Project B will still be chosen because where there is a conflict between NPV and IRR, NPV dominates.

LEASE OR BUY DECISION

Learning is a form of finance whereby an asset can be used within a business without it necessarily bought outright. In this section, we are looking at the problem of evaluating whether leasing is better than outright purchase with borrowed funds in a particular situation.

Thus, where the use of an asset is required for a new project, there are effectively two decisions to be made:

- Is the project worthwhile?
- If so, should the asset be leased or bought with a loan?

The approach preferred by examiners is as follows: if you are asked to evaluate both the project and the finance, then calculate two Net Present Values (NPVs):

- NPV of the project assuming the asset is bought
- NPV of the project assuming the asset is leased.

These NPVs can then be compared to see which is the most attractive and whether the project is worth investing in. If you are told that the project has already been approved and you are asked to evaluate the finance, then calculate the two NPV values:

- NPV of the asset cash flows if bought
- NPV of the leasing cash flows.

Again these can be compared to see which financing method is cheaper. Thus, the method with lower cash flow is preferred.

EVALUATING THE FINANCE OPTION WITHOUT REFERENCE TO THE PROJECT

In most instances, you will be told that the project has already been approved and you are only asked to evaluate the finance option. To do this you need to calculate the next present values of the two sets of financing cash flows for buying and leasing.

For buying the cash flows would be:

- The purchase cost.
- Any residue value.
- Any associated tax implications due to capital allowances.

For leasing the cash flows would be:

- The lease payments
- Tax relief on the lease payments.

Example 5

PCBF Ltd is considering the purchase of a printer for K400 000 cash. Alternatively, the printer can be leased from ICC on a 5-year contract for K110 000 per year. If the printer is bought outrightly, the service and maintenance charges would be K16 000 per annum, whereas the lease charge includes maintenance and servicing.

The salvage value of the printer in 5 years is expected to be nil. The company uses straight-line method of depreciation. The company's tax rate is 30% and the pre-tax cost of debt is 10%.

(a) Calculate the cost of earning, using discounted cash flow method.
(b) Calculate the cost of leasing, using discounted cash flow method
(c) Advise on the option to be adopted. Justify your answer.

Solution

Since this is a financing decision, not a capital budgeting one, the relevant discount rate is the after tax cost of debt. The pre-tax cost of debt is 10%. The after tax cost of debt can be approximated by multiplying this by (1 – tax rate i.e. 10% x (1 – 0.3) = 7%

(a) Owning

Detail	Year 0	Year 1	Year 2	Year 3	Year 4	Year 5
Purchase price	(400000)	-	-	-	-	-
Service charge (16000 x 0.7)	-	(11200)	(11200)	(11200)	(11200)	(11200)
Dep. Tax shield (80000 x 0.3)	-	24000	24000	24000	24000	24000
Net cash flow	-	12800	12800	12800	12.800	12800

Discount factor at 7%	-	0.9346	0.88734	0.8163	0.7629	0.7130
Present value cash flow	(400000)	11963	11180	10449	9765	9126
					NPV	(347517)

b) Leasing

Detail	Year 1	Year 2	Year 3	Year 4	Year 5
Lease payments	(110 000)	(110 000)	(110 000)	(110000)	(110 000)
Tax shield (0.3)	33 000	33 000	33 000	33 000	33 000
Net cash flow	(77 000)	(77 000)	(77 000)	(77 000)	(77 000)
Discount factor 7%	0.9346	0.8734	0.8163	0.7629	0.7130
Present value	(71 964)	(67 252)	(62 855)	(58 743)	(54 901)
				NPV	(347 517)

(c) It is an advantage to lease rather than own. The NPV of cash flows is greater for owning by (K31802).

Note: Tax shield = K110 000 x 0.3 = K33 000 and is treated as positive (or inflow).

- Depreciation tax shield associated with owning the printer must be determined, since depreciation itself is not an actual cash flow.

- Depreciation = $\frac{Cost - Scrap}{Useful\ life}$ = $\frac{400\ 000}{5}$ = K80 000

- Depreciation tax shield K80 000 x 0.3 = K24 000

Alternative solution is as follows:

(a) Owning option

After tax cost of debt = 10% (1 – 0.3) = 7%

Year 0   purchase price   = (400 000)
Year 1 – 5 service charge (16000 x 0.7 x 4.1002)   = (42 922)
Year 1 – 5 Depreciation tax shield (80000 x 0.3
                                          x 4.1002)   =   98 405

                    NPV of owning   K (347 517)

(b) Leasing option

Year 1 – 5 lease payments 110 000 x 4.1002 = (451022)

Year 1 – 5 Tax shield 110 000 x 0.3 x 4.1002 = <u>135 307</u>

NPV of leasing <u>K (315 715)</u>

(c) It is an advantage to lease than own. The NPV of cash flows is greater for owning by K (31 802).

Note that above calculations could easily be worked out using annuities mathematics. See Chapter 8.

Example 6

Jose Ltd must decide whether to buy a new machine for K210 000 000 enter into a service contract at K1500 000 per month for 5 years (option 1) or lease the machine for K40 000 000 each month over a 5 – year period and they purchase it at the end of 5 years for K50 000 000 (option 2) if the company can earn 10% compounded quarterly on its money, should the company buy or lease the machine?

Solution

Here the complications of tax relief and depreciation shield are ignored. Hence the requirement is to determine the present values of each of the options. Since we don't have discount factor, we cannot use NPV techniques.

Option 1: Buying

Total Present Value = PV of initial payment + PV of annuity of K1.5 million.

$$= K210\ 000\ 000 + 1\ 500\ 000 \left[\frac{1 - (1.025)^{-20}}{0.025} \right]$$

$$= 210\ 000\ 000 + 1\ 500\ 000\ (15.58916228)$$

$$= 210,000\ 000 + 23,383,743.42$$

$$= K2\ 33,383,743.40$$

Option 2: Leasing

Total Present Value = PV of lease payments + PV of purchase price

$$= 40\ 000\ 000 \left[\frac{1 - (1 - 025)^{-20}}{0.025} \right] + 50\ 000\ 000\ (1.025)^{-20}$$

$$= 40\ 000\ 000\ (15.58916228) + 50\ 000\ 000\ (0.610270942)$$

$$= 623,566,491.20 + 30,513547.10$$

$$= K654\ 080\ 038.30$$

- Since the present value of buying (K233 383 743.40) is lower than the present value of leasing (K654 080 038.30) buying is a better option.

PROGRESS CLINIC 7

1. The following information relates to two possible capital projects to be undertaken by PCBF Limited. Both projects have an initial capital cost of K400 million and only one can be undertaken.

Expected Profits Year	project x K000	Project y K000
1	160 000	60 000
2	160 000	100 000
3	80 000	180 000
4	40 000	240 000
Estimated resale value at end of year 4:	80 000	80 000

Additional information:

i) Profit is calculated after deducting straight line depreciation.

ii) the cost of capital is 16%

Required

a) Calculate the Net Present Value for both projects.

b) Advice the company which project in your opinion should be undertaken giving reasons for your decision.

c) Explain what is meant by the cost of capital in investment appraisal.

2. ABC Limited is looking to automate one of its production processes in order to produce cash savings and has spent K125 million on a management consultancy exercise. The exercise has identified two alternative two projects that, if installed, would have the following profile and cash savings over a project life of 5 years.

	Project x K000	project y K000
Cost	650 000	750 000
Cash savings year 1	150 000	50 000
2	225 000	100 000
3	275 000	150 000
4	75 000	450 000
5	50 000	300 000

Additional information

a) Project x would have a residual value of K100 million and project y a residual value of K200 million at the end of year 5.

b) All cash flows will arise at the end of the relevant year.

c) The company's cost of capital is 12%

Required

a) Calculate the net present value for each of the two projects

b) Advice ABC Limited which project to invest in clearly stating your reasons.

c) Explain how the expenditure of K125 million on a management consultancy exercise should be treated when appraising the two projects.

3. The following two capital projects involve the purchase,use and final disposal of the two machines A and B.

	Initial cost	Year 1	Year 2	Year 3	Year 4
			Net cash flows		
Machine A	50 000	25 500	24 500	17 000	14000
Machine B	45 000	12 500	15 500	21 000	38 000

Note that year 4 includes scrap values of K5000 for machine A and K4000 for machine B. Which of the two projects should the company under take using?

a)   Net Present Value – using a cost of capital of 22% and 28%
b)   Internal Rate of Return – estimate its value using results in (Q).

4.A company is considering investing in a product which will involve cash investment of K21 million in the year 2010 and K30 million in 2011. After tax cash receipts of K7.5 million in 2012, K9 million in 2013, K10.5 million in 20 14 and 12 million each year thereafter up to 2020. While the project will be viable after 2020, the directors prefer to be prudent and limit all calculations to that time.

Required

a) If the required rate of return is 15%, what will be the Net Present Value of a project? Comment on its acceptability.

b) Is it possible to compute IRR from above information? If yes, find the project's IRR.

5. A company is considering whether to make an investment costing K28 million which would earn K8 000 000 per annum for 3 years. The company expects to make a return of at least 11% per annum. Is the project viable? Use NPV technique.

6. The Net Present Value of a project x at a discount factor 16% is K14 130 000 positive and at 20% is (5840 000) negative. Calculate the present's Internal Rate of Return.

7. Business has K70 000 000 to invest and the estimated net cash returns from each project over a given 6 years are as follows:

Year	project A K000	project B K000	Project C K000
1	25 000	16 000	15 000
2	23 000	18 000	17 000
3	18 000	18 000	17 000
4	14 000	16 000	16 000
5	10 000	16 000	15 000
6	8 000	12 000	10 000

If the discount rate is 12%, which project would be preferable using NPV?

8. A company is trying to decide whether to buy a machine for K13 500 000. The machine creates annual cash savings as follows:

Year	K
1	5000 000
2	8000 000
3	3000 000

Calculate the machine's IRR and comment on its acceptability.

9. A business undertakes high-risk investments and requires a minimum expected rate of return of 17% on its investments. A proposed capital investment has the following expected cash flows.

Year	Kwacha
0	(50 000 000)
1	18 000 000
2	25 000 000
3	20 000 000
4	10 000 000

Required

a) calculate the NPV of the project if the cost of capital is 15%
b) Calculate the NPV of the project if the cost of capital is 20%
c) Use the NPVs you have calculated to estimate the IRR of the present.
d) Recommend, on financial grounds alone, whether this project should go ahead.

CHAPTER 8

ANNUITIES

INTRODUCTION

An annuity is a constant sum of money received or paid each time period for a given total number of periods. In this Chapter, we take a detailed look at annuities. Particular attention must be paid to the difference between an annuity due and an ordinary annuity since computations for the two do differ. More important also is the realization that in the analysis of annuities our main concern is the "number of interest periods" rather than the number of years. Compounding for annuities may be done weekly, monthly, quarterly or indeed semi-annually which means that the right periodic rate must be applied.

However, interest periods need not be affected by the frequency of compounding. Make sure you learn and understand, the techniques of this Chapter as you will need to apply this knowledge in the next two Chapters.
An annuity is a sequence of fixed equal payment or receipt made over uniform time intervals.

The common examples of annuities are weekly or monthly salaries, insurance premiums, house purchase mortgage payments, lease payments, hire purchase payments, etc.

Annuities used in all areas of business and commercial loans are normally repaired with an annuity.

Investment funds are set up to meet fixed future commitments e.g. asset repayments by the payments of an annuity.

Perpetual annuities can be purchased with a single lump – sum payment to enhance pension

TYPES OF ANNUITIES

The common classifications of annuities are:

(1) *Ordinary annuity* – This is an annuity paid at the end of payment interval e.g. At the end of the year. It starts at period interval 1.

(2) *Due annuity* – This is an annuity paid at the beginning of the payment interval e.g. at the beginning of the year. It starts at period 0.

(3) *Annuity certain* – this is an annuity where the term of an annuity may begin and end on fixed dates.

(4) *Contingent annuity* – This is an annuity which depends on some event that cannot be fixed.

(5) *Perpetual annuity* – this is an annuity that carries on indefinitely and it does not have a maturity.

The most common form of an annuity is certain and ordinary, i.e. the annuity will be paid at the end of the payment interval and will begin and end on fixed dates e.g. Most hire purchase contracts will involve the payment of an initial deposit and then equal monthly payments payable at the end of each month up to a fixed date. Personal loans from banks and finance companies are paid off in a similar manner but normally without an initial deposit.

Standard payment or supper annuities schemes can be thought of as two stage annuities. The first stage involves a due certain annuity i.e. regular payments into the fund up to the retirement age and the second stage being the receipt of the contingent annuity i.e. regular receipts until death.

Annuities that are invested are due i.e. They are paid in advance of the interval e.g. a savings scheme paid as an annuity with a bank or building society will not be deemed to have started payment has been made.

ANNUITY FACTORS

An annuity factor for interval payments n at interest rate r can be read off from the annuity tables directly or calculated from an electronic calculator using the following formula:

$$\text{Annuity factor} = \frac{1}{r}\left(1 - \frac{1}{(1+r)^n}\right) \text{ or } \left(\frac{1-(1+r)^{-n}}{r}\right)$$

Where n = Number of payment intervals (periods)

r = Interest rate for the period expressed as a proportion.

Example: Find the annuity factors of the following using the formula.

a) n = 4, r = 10%   b) n = 3, r = 9.5%

c) For 20 years at a rate of 25%.

Solution

a) $\left(\dfrac{1-(1+0.1)^{-4}}{0.1}\right)$

= 3.170

b) $\left(\dfrac{1-(1+0.095)^{-3}}{0.095}\right)$

= 2.508906821

= 2.509

c) $\left(\dfrac{1-(1+0.25)^{-20}}{0.25}\right)$

$= 3.95388314$

$= 3.954$

NOTE: Generally, *annuity factors are always greater than 0 because they are cumulative figures.*

PRESENT VALUE OF AN ANNUITY

The most common types of annuities are:

1. An ordinary annuity certain

2. Annuity due certain

Generally the present value of an annuity is the sum of the present values of each payment over a given period of time.

Formula for present value an Ordinary Annuity.

Is given by
$$A = R\left(\dfrac{1-(1+r)^{-n}}{r}\right)$$

Where
    A = Present value of an ordinary annuity
    R = Payment per payment period
    n = Number of periods payment is made
    r = interest rate per period

The derivation of the above formula is as follows:

Consider an annuity of n payments of R each, where interest rate per period is r and the first payment is due one period from now. The graphical illustration of the above statement is as follows:

Period

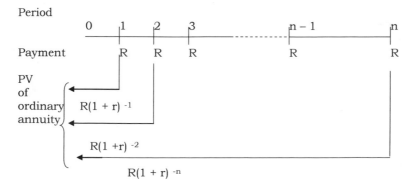

From above the present value A of the annuity is given by:

$A = R (1 + r)^{-1} + R (1 + r)^{-2} + \ldots\ldots\ldots + R(1 + r)^{-n}$

This is a geometric series on n terms with the first term $R (1 + r)^{-1}$ and common ratio $(1 + r)^{-1}$

Hence $A = \dfrac{R(1 + r)^{-1} (1 + r)^{-n}}{1 - (1 + r)^{-1}}$ Note: To work out this you need to use $(1+r)^{-1} = \dfrac{1}{1+r}$

$= \dfrac{R(1/(1+r)-(1+r)^{-n}}{1 - (1/1+r)}$

$= R(1/1+r)-(1+r)^{-n} \times (1+r)/r$

$= \dfrac{R (1 - (1 + r)^{-n})}{r}$

$= \dfrac{R (1 - (1 + r)^{-n})}{r}$

Alternative but similar formula is

$PV = \dfrac{A}{r} \left[1 - \dfrac{1}{(1 + r)^{n}} \right]$

Where

>PV = present value
>A = Annuity
>n = Number of periods
>r = Interest rate during the period

PRESENT VALUE OF AN ANNUITY DUE

An annuity due is one where payment is made at the beginning of the period.

As with an ordinary annuity, the graphical representation is as follows:

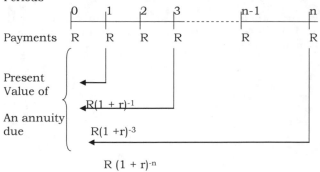

Thus, the formula for present value of an annuity due may be written as follows:

$$A = R + \dfrac{R(1 - (1 + r)^{-n}}{r}$$

Where

  A = present value of an annuity due
  R = payment per payment period
  n = Number of periods payment is made
  r = Interest rate per period

Example 1

What is the present value of K4000 000 per annum for years 1 to 4 at a discount rate of 10% per annum.

Solution

Above is an ordinary annuity certain

$A = R \dfrac{(1 - (1 + r)^{-n})}{r}$ Where R = K4000 000
                                                    n = 4
                                                    r = 0.1

$A = K4000\ 000 \left[\dfrac{1 - (1 + 0.1)^{-4}}{0.1} \right]$

$= K4000\ 000 \left[\dfrac{1 - (1 - 1)^{-4}}{0.1} \right]$

$= K4000\ 000 \times 3.169865446$

$= K12, 679,461.79$

NOTE: *K4000 000 per year for four (4) years gives K16 000 000 but this K16 000 000 is only worth about K12, 679,461.79 now.*

> Further, present value of an annuity = Annuity X Annuity Factor

Example 2

Given an interest rate of 6% compounded annually, find the present value of the following annuity: K50 000 due at the end of year for 5 years, and K125 000 due thereafter at the end of each year for 3 years.

Solution

This is an ordinary annuity certain and the present value is found by summing the present value of all payments as follows:

K50 000 $(1 + 0.6)^{-1}$ + K50 000 $(1 + 0.06)^{-2}$ + K50 000 $(1 + 0.06)^{-3}$
  K50 000 $(1 + 0.06)^{-4}$ + K50 000 $(1 + 0.06)^{-5}$ + K125 000 $(1 + 0.06)^{-6}$

+ K125 000 $(1 + 0.06)^{-7}$ + K125 000 $(1 + 0.06)8$ = K50 000 (0.943396

+ K50 000 (0.889946) + K50 000 (0.839619) + K50 000 (0.792094) + K50 000

(0.747258) + K125 000 (0.0504961) + K125 000 (0.665057) + K125 000

(0.627412) = K47169.8 + K44499.82 + K41980.95 + K39604.70 + K37362.9

+ K88120.125 + K83132.125 + K78426.5 = K460296.90.

Alternatively, we can simplify the above work by considering the payments to be an annuity of K125 000 for 8 years, minus an annuity of K75 000 each (Note: K125 000 – K50 000 = K75 000).
Thus, the present value is:

$$K125\ 000 \left(\frac{1-(1+0.06)^{-8}}{0.06} \right) - K75\ 000 \left[\frac{1-(1+0.06)^{-5}}{0.06} \right]$$

= K125 000 (6.209793811) – K75 000 (4.21363785)

= K776224.2264 – K315925.2839

= K460 296.9425

= k460 296.94

Example 3

A company wishes to lease temporary office space for a period of 6 months. The rental fee K50 000 a month payable in advance. Suppose that the company wants to make a lump-sum payment at the beginning of the rental period to cover all rental fees due over the 6-month period. If money is worth 9% compounded monthly, how much should the payment be?

Solution

Above is an annuity due and can be considered as an initial payment of K50 000 followed by an ordinary annuity of K50 000 for 5 periods.

Periodic rate = $\frac{9\%}{12}$ = 0.75% = 0.0075

n = 5, R = K50 000

$$= K50\ 000 + K50\ 000 \left[\frac{1-(1+0.0075)^{-5}}{0.0075} \right]$$

= K50 000 + K50 000 (4.889439612)

= K50 000 + K244, 471.9806

= K294, 471.98

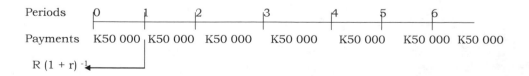

134

CALCULATING THE REQUIRED ANNUITY

Bearing in mind that the present value of an annuity multiplied by annuity factor, then the required annuity can be obtained by rearranging the formula provided the present value and the annuity factors are known or can be calculated from the given information.

> Thus required annuity = $\dfrac{\text{Present value of an annuity}}{\text{Annuity factor}}$

Or

> $R = \dfrac{Ar}{(1 - (1 + r)^{-n}}$

Where present value of an annuity is obtained by summing the present values of all payments

$$\text{Annuity factor} = \left(\dfrac{1 - (1 + r)^{-n}}{r} \right)$$

Example 4

A bank grants a loan of K3000 000 at 7% per annum. The borrower is to repay the loan in 10 equal annual installments. How much must she pay each year.

Solution

Since the bank pays out the loan money now, the present value of the loan is K3000 000. The annual repayments can be thought of as an annuity.

Thus, required annuity = $\dfrac{\text{present value of annuity}}{\text{Annuity factor}}$

Annuity factor at n = 10, r = 7%

Is $(1 - (1 + 0.07)^{-10}) = 7.023581541$

Therefore $\dfrac{\text{K3000 000}}{7.023581541}$

$= \underline{\text{K427, 142.51}}$

The loan repayments are therefore K427, 132.51 per annum

Example 5

Mweemba wants to buy a car. This will cost him K45 000 000 in two year's time. He has decided to set aside an equal installments each quarter until he has enough) the amount he needs). Assuming he can earn interest in his Zambia National Building society account at 5% per annum, how much does he need to set aside each year? Assume the first amount is set aside one period from now.

Solution

Mweemba needs K45 000 000 in two year's time present value of K45 000 000

= K45 000 000 $(1 + 0.05)^{-2}$

= K40 816 326.53

Annuity factor at n = 2, r = 5% is

$$\frac{(1 - (1 + 0.05)^{-2}}{0.05}$$

= 1.859410431

Required annuity = $\frac{K40\ 816\ 326.53}{1.859410431}$

= K21, 951,219.51

Thus, Mweemba needs to set aside K21, 951, 219.51 per year to enable him his K45 000 000 worth dream car.

NOTE: *K21, 951, 219.51 per year for 2 years amounts to K43 902 439.02 which K45 000 000. How is he going to manage to pay the required amount? Oh! The difference is earned from his account at ZNBS. So about K1, 097 560.98 is the interest he will earn in 2years at 5% interest per annum.*

Example 6

What value would have been built up if Mweemba had saved K21, 951,219.51 per annum for two years at interest rate of 5% with the first payment made at end of year 1.

Solution

This is an example of an ordinary annuity using a time line, this can be presented a s follows:

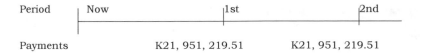

Period	Now		1st		2nd	
Payments		K21, 951, 219.51		K21, 951, 219.51		

The value of the fund at the end of year 2 is: K21, 951, 219.51 + K21, 951, 219.51 (1.05). Above forms a geometric progression, hence be determined using sum of a geometric progression with a = K21, 951, 219.51, R = 1.05, n = 2

$S_n = \dfrac{K21, 951, 219.51 (1.05^2 - 1)}{1.05 - 1}$

$= K45, 000, 000$

This proves that if Mweemba saves K21, 951, 219.51 per annum, it will amount to K45, 000 000.

Example 7

John has taken out a K30 000 000 mortgage over 25 years. Interest is to be charged at 12% per annum. Calculate the monthly repayment.

Solution

Present value of the mortgage = K30 000 000 since a mortgage is taken now hence cannot be discounted.

The annuity factor is:

$$\left[\frac{1 - (1 + r)^{-n}}{r} \right]$$

Where n = 25
r = 0.12

$$\left[\frac{1 - (1.12)^{-25}}{0.12} \right]$$

$= 7.843139112$

Annuity (Annual payments) $= \dfrac{PV}{AF} = \dfrac{K30\ 000\ 000}{7.843139108}$

$= K3824999.10$

Monthly repayment $= \dfrac{K3824999.10}{12}$

$= 318, 749.92$

Alternatively,using sum of geometric progression. Find future value of mortgage

$= K30\ 000\ 000\ (1.12)^{25}$

$= K51\ 000\ 1932.20$

Sum of repayments

A = Annual payment, R = 1.12, n = 25

Sum of repayments $= A(1.12^{25} - 1) = 133.333870\ 1A$

Sum of repayments = final value of mortgage 133.3338701A = K5 1000 1932.20

$A = \dfrac{K51000\ 1932.\ 20}{133.3338701}$

= K3, 824999.09

Monthly payment = $\dfrac{K3824999.09}{12}$

= K318, 749.92

CALCULATING THE REQUIRED NUMBER OF INSTALLMENTS

Sometimes it is necessary to calculate the required number of installments to complete a given financial obligation In other words, we may be asked to determine n given r , A, present value of an annuity and the future value of an annuity. Here is an instance where the use of logarithms and rules of indices becomes indispensable. Check out the following example.

Example 8

Suppose a bank grants a loan of K3000 000 at 7% per annum. The borrower is to repay the loan by paying an annuity of K427 132.51. How many installments does she need to fully repay the loan?

Solution

Above is the same question as in example 3 above and the solution we need is to find that the borrower needs to make 10 equal annual installments.

Annuity = $\dfrac{\text{Present value of an annuity}}{\text{Annuity factor}}$

Present value of the loan is K3000 000, Annuity = K427 132.51

Therefore K427 132.51 = K3000 000 $\left[\dfrac{1-(1.07)^{-n}}{0.07}\right]$

K427 132.51 = K3000 000 X $\dfrac{0.07}{(1-(1.07)^{-n}}$

K427 132.51 = $\dfrac{K210\ 000}{[1-(1.07)^{-n}]}$

= $\dfrac{K427\ 132.51\ (1-(1.07)^{-n}}{K427\ 132.51}$

= $\underline{K210\ 000}$

K427 132.51

$= 1 - (1.07)^{-n} = 0.491650705$

$= 1.07)^{-n} = 0.508349295$

$= \dfrac{1}{(1.07)^n} = 0.508349295$

$= 1 = 0.508349295 \, (1.07)^n$

$1 \, 967151346 = (1.07)^n$

$\text{Log } 1.96715346 = n \log (1.07)$

$n = \dfrac{\log 1.967151346}{\log 1.07}$

$= \dfrac{0.293837774}{0.029383777}$

$= 10.00000014$
$= 10$

Therefore the loan can be discharged in 10 equal annual installments of K427 132.51 each.

AMORTIZATION ANNUITY

If an amount of money is borrowed over a period of time, one way of repaying the debt is by an amortization annuity. An amortization annuity consists of regular i.e. ordinary and certain in which each payment accounts for both

repayments of capital and interest. The debt is said to be amortized if this method is used.

Many of the types of loans offered by banks and building societies for house purchased are of this type where it is known as a repayment mortgage.

AMORTIZATION SCHEDULE

An amortization schedule is a specification, period by period (normally year by year) of the state of the debt. It is usual to show for each year the following:

(d) Amount of debt outstanding at beginning of year.
(e) Interest paid
(f) Annual payment, and optionally
(g) Amount of principal repaid

NOTE: *that for examination purposes, a schedule would only be asked if the period was relatively short: for example, up to 5 or 6 time periods*

Example 9

Find the annual repayment on a building society loan of K40 000 000 over five years at 12% per annum. Prepare a schedule to show the stat of the debt at each period.

Solution

Required annuity = $\dfrac{\text{present value of the annuity}}{\text{Annuity factor}}$

Present values of loan = K40 000 000

Annuity factor = $\dfrac{(1 - (1 + 0.12)^{-5})}{0.12}$

$= 3.06047762$

Thus required annuity = $\dfrac{\text{K40 000 000}}{3.6047762}$

$= \text{K11 096 389.28}$

Alternatively, R = $\dfrac{Ar}{1 - (1 + r)^{-n}}$ = $\dfrac{40\,000\,000\,(0.12)}{(1 - (1.12)^{-5}}$ = K11096389.28

Amortization Schedule

Period	Outstanding principal at beginning of period K	Interest due k	Payment (annuity) k	Principal repaid at end of period k
1	40 000 000	4 800 000	11 096 389.28	6 296 389.28
2	33 703 610.72	4 044 433.286	11 096 389.28	7 051 955.994
3	26 651 654.74	3 198 198.568	11 096 389.28	7 898 190.712
4	18 753 464.02	2 250 415.682	11 096 389.28	8.845 973.598
5	9 907 490. 422	1 188 898.851	11 096 389.28	9 907 490.429
Total		1 581 946.38	55 481 946.40	40 000 000.02

Notes:

1. Interest due = 12% of outstanding principal at beginning of period.

2. Annual payment is the required annuity.

3. Principal repaid = period payment – interest due.

4. New outstanding principal = outstanding principal earlier + principal repaid at end of period.

5. The debt is cleared by the end of year 5 as shown by the total for principal repaid column.

Example 10

A debt of K16.2 million with interest of 6% compounded semi annually is to be amortized by semi annual payments of K4050 000 each, the first due in 6 months, together with a final partial payment if necessary. Construct a schedule. Find independently, the outstanding principal just after the 3rd payment.

Solution

$$K4050\ 000\ \frac{(1 - (1.03)^{-n})}{0.03} = K16\ 200\ 000$$

$$\frac{(1 - (1.03)^{-n})}{0.03} = 4$$

$$(1 - (1.03)^{-n}) = 0.12$$

$$(1.03)^{-n} = 0.88$$

Using logs n = 4.327

Hence four (4) full payments are required.

SCHEDULE

Period	outstanding Principal at start of period	interest due on principal at end of period	payment	principal repaid at end of period
1	16 200 000	486 000	4050 000	3564 000
2	12 636 000	379 080	4050 000	3670920
3	8 965 080	268 952.4	4050 000	3781047.6
4	5 184 032.4	155 520.97	4050 000	3894479.03
5	1 289 55.37	38186.60	1328 239.97	1289553.37
Total		1328 239.97	17528 239.97	16 200 00

Notes to calculations

1. interest due = outstanding principal X interest rate of 3%
2. period payment is the required annuity
3. principal repaid = period payment – interest due
4. outstanding principal = outstanding principal earlier + interest due - Payment

Alternatively,

The required outstanding principal may be found without first determining the final (partial) payment from the time line.

K16.2 million
   Payment

Interest period   1   2   3   4   5
              K4050 000   K4050 000   K4050 000   K4050 000

The outstanding principal P just after the 3rd payment is

$$P = K16200\,000\,(1.03)^3 - K4050\,000 \left[\frac{(1.03)^3 - 1}{0.03} \right]$$

$$= K16200\,000\,(1.09272) - K4050\,000\,(3.0909)$$

$$= K1702177.4 - K12518145$$

$$= \underline{K5184032.40}$$

Example 11

A debtor is to amortise a K100 000 000 house loan by making equal payments at the end of each month for 6 months. If the interest is at 12% compounded monthly:

(a) Find the amount of each payment
(b) Find the finance charge
(c) Prepare an amortisation schedule
(d) How much would have remained to be paid after the debtor has made his 4th payment?
(e) How would a debtor and lender use the amortisation schedule with regards to the above transaction.

Solution

(a) $A = K100\,000\,000$, $r = \frac{12\%}{12} = 10\% = 0.01$, $n = 6$, $R = ?$

       Using $R = \dfrac{Ar}{1 - (1 + r)^{-n}}$

           $= \dfrac{100\,000\,000\,(0.01)}{1 - (1.01)^{-6}}$

           $= \dfrac{1000\,000}{0.057954764}$

           $= K17{,}254{,}836.89$ as the required payment each month.

(b)   The finance charge is the difference between the total payments and the borrowed amount. Thus, finance charge $= nR - A$

$$= 6(17,254, 836.89) - 100\ 000\ 000$$

$$= 103\ 529\ 021.30 - 100\ 000\ 000$$

$$= K3\ 529\ 021.30$$

(c)   Amortisation schedule

Period	Principal outstanding at beginning of period	Interest per period	Payment at end of period	Principal repaid at end of period
1	100 000 000	1000 000	17 254 836.89	16 254836.89
2	83 7451.6311	837 451.6311	17 254 836.89	16 41385.26
3	67 327777.85	67 3277.7785	17 254 836.89	16 581559.11
4	50 746218.74	507462.1874	17 254 836.89	16 747374.70
5	33 998844.04	339988.4404	17 254 836.89	16 914848.45
6	17 083995.59	170839.9559	17 254 836.89	17 083996.93
Total		3,529,020	103 529 021.30	100 000 001.3

Notes: 1. Interest per period is 1% of outstanding principal at beginning
2. Payment = required annuity
3. Principal repaid = payment – interest per period
4. New principal outstanding at beginning = outstanding principal in earlier period – principal repaid at end of period.

(d)   Principal outstanding after 4th payment is K33 998 844.04. (you can confirm this by use of a formula with n = 2 because the figures are reducing).

(e)   It helps both the debtor and lender to know how much has already been paid, how much has remained to be paid interest charge per period and the periodic payments required to fully pay off the debt.

SINKING FUNDS

A sinking fund can be defined as an annuity invested in order to meet a known commitment at some future date.

Sinking funds are commonly used for the following purposes:

a) Repayment of debt

b) Provide funds for purchase of a new asset when the old is fully depreciated

SINKING FUND SCHEDULE

The sinking fund schedule has a standard presentation designed to show for each year the following:

a)   For debt, the outstanding debt and interest paid
b)   For the, the regular payment, interest earned and amount in fund.

Now work through the following examples to fully understand the techniques of sinking funds theory.

Example 12

A company has just bought an asset with a life of four years. At the end of four years, a replacement asset will cost K12 000 000 and the company has decided to provide for this future commitment by setting up a sinking fund into which equal annual investment will be made, starting at year 1 (one year from now) interest at 12% per annum.

Calculate the annual investment and construct a sinking fund schedule to prove that after 4 years the company would have K12 000 000.

Solution

We illustrate the time line where KA = Equal annual investment.

Period	year 0	year 1	year 2	year 3	year 4	
Payments	Now	1st	2nd	3rd	4th	end

A_____ X $(1.12)^3$

A_____ X⁺ A $(1.12)^2$

_____ X A $(1.12)^1$

(Year 0)   No payment
(Year 1)   The first year's investment will grow to KA X $(1.12)^3$
(Year 2)   The second year's investment will grow to KA X $(1.12)^2$
(Year 3)   Third year's investment will grow to KA X (1.12)
Year 4)   The fourth year's investment will remain KA

The value of the fund at the end of 4 years is as follows:

A + A (1.12) + A(1.12^2) + A(1.12^3) which is a geometric progression with A = A, R = 1.12, n = 4
The value of the sinking fund at the end of year 4 is K1200 000 (given in the question) therefore:

K12 000 000 = A $\underline{(1.12^4 - 1)}$
                      1.12 -1

K12 000 000 = A $\underline{(1.57351936 - 1)}$
                        0.12

K12 000 000 = A (4.779328)

∴ A = $\dfrac{K12\ 000\ 000}{4.779328}$

= K2, 510,813.236

= K2, 510,813.24

Therefore 4 investments each of K2510813.24 should therefore be enough to allow the company to replace the asset.

Alternatively, the required annual investment could be found as:

Annual investment = $\dfrac{\text{present value of the amount}}{\text{Annuity factor}}$

Present value of K12 000 000 = K12 000 000 $(1.12)^{-4}$

= K7, 626,216.941

Annuity factor = $\left[\dfrac{1-(1.12)^{-4}}{0.12}\right]$ = 3.037349347

Annual investment = $\dfrac{K7,626,216.941}{3.037349347}$

= K2,510,813.235

The sinking fund schedule is therefore as follows:

Year	Payment	Total in fund	Interest	Amount in fund At end of year
1	2,510,813.235	2 510 813.235	301,297.5882	2 812 110.823
2	2,510,813.235	5 322 924.058	638 750.887	5 961 674.945
3	2,510813.235	8 472 488.18	1016 698.582	9 489 186.762
4	2,510,813.235	12 000 000	-	-

The sinking fund schedule confirms that if investments each of K2510 813.24 should be enough to allow the company to replace the asset.

Notes to calculations above.

1. Payments = required annuity
2. interest received = 12% of total in fund
3. Total in fund = amount in fund at year end + payment
4. Amount in fund at year end = total in fund + interest

Example 13

Mr. Lublinkof of Mubuyu Farms has just bought a combine harvester which has a life of 10 years. At the end of 10 years a replacement combine harvester will cost K100 000 000 and he would like to provide for this future commitment by setting up a sinking fund into which equal annual investments will be made, starting now. The will earn interest at 10% per annum.

a) Calculate the annual investment
b) Set up a sinking fund schedule
c) Using the schedule determine how much the fund will be worth just after the 6th payment.

Solution

Required annual investment = $\frac{\text{present value of K100 000 000}}{\text{Annuity factor}}$

Present value of K100 000 000 = K100 000 000 $(1.1)^{-10}$

Annuity factor = $\left(\frac{1-(1.1)^{-10}}{0.1}\right)$ = 6.144567106

Required annual investment = $\frac{\text{K38, 554328.94}}{6.144567106}$

= K6, 274,539.487

Thus, the farmer must invest K6, 274,539.89 annually.

Year	*payment*	*Total in fund*	*interest earned*	*Amount in fund at end of year*
1	6 274 539.49	6,274,539.49	627,453.949	6,901,993.44
2	6 274 539.49	13,176,532.93	1,317,653.29	14,494,186.22
3	6 274 539.49	20,768,725.71	2,076,872.57	22,845,598.28
4	6 274 539.49	29,120,137.77	2,912,013.78	32,032,151.55
5	6 274 539.49	38,306,691.63	3,830,669.10	42,137,360.14
6	6 274 539.49	48,411,899.63	4,841,189.90	53,253,089.59
7	6 274 539.49	59,527,629.08	5,952,762.91	65,480,391.99
8	6 274 539.49	71,754,931.48	7,175,493.15	78,930,424.63
9	6 274 539.49	85,204,964.12	8,520,496.41	93,725,460.53
10	6 274 539.49	100 000 000 .00	-	-

Notes to calculations above

1. payment – required investment
2. interest received = 10% of the total in fund
3. Total in fund = amount in fund + interest received

d) after the sixth payment the fund will be worth K59,527,629.08

Example 14

What is the maturity value of a fund paying 9.5% into which 5 advance annual payment of K2, 400 000 are made. Confirm your answer by way of a sinking fund schedule.

Solution

Year	Payment	Total in fund	Interest	Amount in Fund at year end
1	2,400,000	2,400,000	228 000	2,628,000
2	2,400,000	5,028,000	477,660	5,505,660
3	2,400,000	7,905,660	751,037.70	8, 656, 697.70
4	2,400,000	11,056,697.70	1,050,386.28	12,107,083.98
5	2,400,000	14,507,083.98	1,378,172.98	15,885,256.96

Notes to calculations

1. interest received = 9.5% of total in fund
2. Amount in fund at year end = Total in fund + interest
3. Total in fund = amount in fund at year end + payment

Thus, the maturity value in the fund is K15, 885,256.96

As an exercise, what alternative method can you use to get the maturity value in the fund?

Note that above is an annuity due.

SINKING FUND METHOD OF DEPRECIATION

One reason for depreciating an asset is to take proper account of its replacement. Thus one can consider the periodic book payments in respect of depreciation, the depreciation charge, as forming a pool that, at the end of the asset's useful life, will fund a replacement or alternative.

The sinking fund method of depreciation considers the depreciation charge payments as being available for investment into a fund (a depreciation fund, paying a market rate of interest) which will mature to some predetermined value. The book value of the respective asset at the end of any year can be determined by subtracting the current amount in fund from the original book of asset.

DEPRECIATION SCHEDULE

A depreciation schedule can be set up showing for each year the following.

   a) payment into the fund (depreciation charge)
   b) interest earned
   c) amount in fund
   d) current book value of asset

Example 15

A machine valued atK12 500 000, with a six year life, is estimated to have a scrap value of K450 000. If the deprecation funds earns 8%.

   a) Use the sinking fund based on an ordinary annuity to find the annual deposit into the fund (depreciation charge).
   b) Prepare a depreciation schedule
   c) During what year does the value of the machine reach 50% of its original value?

Solution

a) The difference between the original value of the machine and its scrap value:

   K12 500 000 – K450 000 = K12 050 000 which must be the value of the depreciation fund after 6 years. Interest paid to fund is 8%.

Thus we have to calculate the required annual payment into the depreciation fund.

Using the sum of the geometric progression

$$S_n = \frac{A(R^n - 1)}{r},$$

Where S_n = K12, 050,000

               R = 1.08

               n = 6

               r = 0.08

Substituting in the formula we have:

K12 050 000 = $\dfrac{A(1.08^6 - 1)}{0.08}$

K12 050 000 = $\dfrac{A(0.586874322)}{0.08}$

K12 050 000 = A (7.335929037)

:. A = $\underline{K12050000}$
       7.33592999037

= K1, 642,600.404

Alternatively, we can use the required annuity formula below to determine the depreciation charge.

Required annuity = $\underline{\text{present value of the amount}}$
                        Annuity factor

Present value of K12 050 000 is K12 050 000 $(1.08)^{-6}$ = K7, 593,544.004

Annuity factor = $\underline{1-(1.08)^{-6}}$ = 4.622879664
                        0.08

Thus, required annuity = $\underline{K7, 593,544.004}$
                              4.622879664

= K1, 642,600.404

Thus, one has a choice to make depending on whether one is more comfortable with sum of geometric progression method or the annuity method as both yields the same figure. So the choice is yours.

Thus, annual depreciation charge is K1, 642,600.40

b) The depreciation schedule is as follows

Year	Depreciation charge	Amount in fund	Interest earned	Book value
0	0	0	0	12, 500 000
1	1,642,600.40	1,642,600.40	0	10,857,399.60
2	1,642,600.40	3, 416, 608.83	131,408.03	9,083,391.17
3	1,642,600.40	5,332,537.94	273,328.71	7,167,462.06
4	1,642,600.40	7,401,741.38	426,603.04	5.098.258.62
5	1,642,600.40	9,636,481.09	592,139.31	2,863,518.91
6	1,642,600.40	12, 04999.64	770,918.49	450,000.02

Notes to calculations

1. interest earned = 8% of the amount in fund previously

2. book value (current) = Book value previously – depreciation charge – interest earned

3. Amount in fund = Depreciation charge + amount in fund previously + interest earned currently.

4. It can be seen that after the 6th year payment amount in fund = K12, 049,999.64 and the book value = K450 000.02.

These are the K12 500 000 and K50 000 respectively. The differences arise because of rounding off number to two decimal places.

c) 50% of the original value of the machine is K12 500 000 divide by 2 = K6 250 000 and from the schedule, this value is first reached during the 4th year. (5,098,258.62)

Note: 75% of the original value is K12500 000 X 0.75 = K9, 375,000 which is first reached during the 2nd year (K9.083, 391.17)

Note: lower figures are picked because book values are decreasing.

PERPETUITIES

Perpetuities are annuities that continue indefinitely. They have no maturity because n = ∞ (infinite). The best example are the consoles which are bonds that were issued by the British government during the second World War which will continue paying the holders until Jesus' second coming.

PRESENT VALUE OF PERPETUITY

The present value of perpetuity is calculated using the following formula.

$$PV = \frac{A}{r}$$

Where A = Annual payment
r = interest rate

Example 16

Find the present value of K12, 000,000 per annum in perpetuity at an interest rate of 7.5%.

Solution

$$PV = \frac{A}{r} \qquad A = K12, 000,000$$
$$r = 0.075$$

Thus, $PV = \frac{K12, 000,000}{0.075}$

= K160, 000,000

Thus, the present value of K12, 000 000 per annum in perpetuity at an interest rate of 7.5% is K160, 000,000

PROGRESS CLINIC 8

1. Mr. Kalaki has just received his gratuity as a Member of Parliament amounting to K60 million. He wishes to invest K50 million of the gratuity. He is now faced with a 2 choice between

   two investment opportunities A and B. Capital outlay for each is K50 million. A is estimated to yield an annuity of K20 million at the end of each year receivable every after 5 years. B yields K11 million receivable at the end of year perpetuity. If the discount rate is estimated at 20% for Mr. Kalaki:

   a)   Evaluate the two investment opportunities using the Net Present Value technique.

   b)   Recommend with a reason which one of the two investment opportunities Mr. Kalaki should choose.

2. Find the present value of an annuity of K30 000 000 for 5 years using compound interest at 4% per annum, the first receipt being in one year's time.

3. The terms for a 5 year lease agreement are that K10 million must be paid at the beginning of the first year, to be followed by four equal installments at the beginning of years two, three, four and five at a discount rate of 8%. If the present value of the four equal payments is K26 496 000. What is the total amount to be paid during the lease?

4. Find the annuity factors correct to 4 decimal places for each of the following using annuity formula.

   a)   n = 10, r = 12%
   b)   For 20 years at an interest rate of 20% per annum
   c)   For 6 years at an interest rate of 10% compounded quarterly
   d)   For 3 years at an interest rate of 15% compounded monthly.

5. Determine the present values of the following transactions:

   a)   A bank grants a mortgage loan worth K100 000 00 to Mr. Nyumba Yanga. Interest is to be charged at 10%.

   b)   Mr. Nyumba Yanga wished to serve each annual payments into an account giving 10% interest per annum in order to have K100 000 000 at the end of 12 years.

6. How much need to be invested now at 5% to yield an annual income of K4 million in perpetuity?

CHAPTER 9

BONDS

INTRODUCTION

A bond is a paper that the issuer undertakes to redeem from the buyer or holder at some future date called *maturity date* or at a series of future dates including final maturity.

A bond that the issuer undertakes to redeem from the buyer or holder at a stated amount or maturity is called a pure discount bond. (No payment of interest).

A bond that the issuer undertakes to redeem from the buyer or holder at stated amount at a series of future date including final maturity is called coupon bond. (Interest payment + original amount is paid).

The essence is that from the buyer of the bond, the amount paid to begin with must be lower than the amount to be received in future, for the buyer the bond yield is the internal rate of return of the transaction.

For the issuer, the essence is that the funds used could be invested in projects that would give a higher yield than the redemption rate of the bond

Thus, in a bond transaction, there are two parties namely bond issuer i.e. the borrower and bond holder i.e. the lender.

In this chapter, we take a look at detailed analysis of bonds. Specifically, we will define the key terms and concepts, and carry out a number of calculations involving coupon and zero bonds.

KEY TERMS IN THE ANALYSIS OF BONDS

1. *Par value* – This is the stated face value of the bond. It represents the amount of money that the bond issuer borrows and promises to repay on the maturity date.

2. *Coupon payment* – this is the interest paid regularly i.e. year, or half-yearly. It is expressed in Kwacha terms. It can be calculated using the following.

> Coupon payment = coupon rate x face value

3. *Coupon interest rate*: This is the coupon payment expressed as a percentage of the par value. It is calculated using the following:

> Coupon rate = $\dfrac{\text{Coupon payment x 100}}{\text{Par value}}$

Example

Find the coupon rate for a bond with K1000 par value and which pays 100 in interest each year.

Coupon rate = $\dfrac{\text{coupon payment x 100}}{\text{Par value}}$

$\dfrac{\text{K100 x 100}}{\text{K1000}}$ = 10%

PURE DISCOUNT OR ZERO COUPON BOND

This is a bond where the issuer promises to make a single payment at some future date. The single payment made in future is the face value of the bond. The bond is sold at a discount less the face value.

PRESENT VALUE OF A PURE DISCOUNT BOND

The present value of a pure discount bond is simply the present value of the face, value of the bond and is calculated using the following:

$$P = F (1 + r)^{-n}$$

Where P = present value or purchase price or market price of a bond.
F = face value or maturity value or par value
r = coupon rate expressed as a proportion
n = maturity period in years
$(1 + r)^{-n}$ = discount factor

Example 1

Suppose GRZ issued 3 years bond with a face value of K100 000 000. What is the present value for an investor who requires a yield of 15% per annum i.e. how much should the investor invest today in order to get K100 000 000 in 3 years time if his yield rate is 15% compounded annually?

Solution

This is a pure discount bond where the investor has to pay less than the face value of the bond.

Here   F = K100 000 000
       P = ?
       r = 0.15
       n = 3
Using P = F $(1 + r)^{-n}$

      = K100 000 000 $(1 + 0.15)^{-3}$

= K100 000 000 (1.15) $^{-3}$

= K100 000 000 X 0.657516232

= <u>K65, 751, 623.24</u>

Thus, our investor should part away with K65, 751,623.24 today so as to receive K100 000 000 after 3 years. He will make a profit of K34, 248,376.76.

CALCULATING THE YIELD RATE

Example 2

If GRZ were selling the bonds in the above for K60 000 000, compute the yield rate.

Solution

Here P = K60 000 000
F = K100 000 000
n = 3
r = ?

Using $P = F(1 + r)^{-n}$

K60 000 000 = K100 000 000 $(1 + r)^{-3}$

K60 000 000 = K100 000 000 $(1 + r)^{-3}$

Dividing by K100 000 000 On both sides

$0.6 = (1 + r)^{-3}$

Taking $(1 + r)^{-3}$ to be $\dfrac{1}{(1 + r)^3}$

We have $0.6 = \dfrac{1}{(1 + r)^3}$

$0.6 (1 + r)^3 = 1$

$(1 + r)^3 = \dfrac{1}{0.6}$

$(1 + r)^3 = 1.666666667$ taking the cube root on both sides.

$1 + r)^3 = 1.666666667$

Taking the cube root on both sides

$1 + r = \sqrt[3]{1.666666667}$

$1 + r = 1.185631102$

$$r = 1.185631102 - 1$$

$$= 0.185631101$$

$$= \underline{18.56\%}$$

CALCULATION OF THE REQUIRED NUMBER OF YEARS

Example 3

How long would it take a GRZ bond with a face value of K100 000 000, at 18.56% if its market price is K60 000 000?

Solution

Here P = K60 000 000
     F = K100 000 000
     r = 0.1856
     n = ?

Using $P = F (1 + r)^{-n}$

K60 000 000 = K100 000 000 $(1 + 0.186)^{-n}$

K60 000 000 = K100 000 000 $(1.1856)^{-n}$

Dividing by K100 000 000 on both sides

$0.6 = (1.1856)^{-n}$

Taking $(1.1856)^{-n}$ to be $\dfrac{1}{(1.1856)^{n}}$

We have $0.6 = \dfrac{1}{(1.1856)^{n}}$

$0.6 = (1.1856)^{n} = 1$

$(1.1856)^{n} = \dfrac{1}{0.6}$

$(1.1856) n = 1.666666667$

Using logarithms

$n \log 1.1856 = \log 1.666666667$

$n = \dfrac{\log 1.666666667}{\log 1.1856}$

$= \dfrac{0.221848749}{0.07393919}$

$= 3.000421684$

$= \underline{3 \text{ years}}$

COUPON BOND

These are bonds that the issuer undertakes to redeem from the holder at a stated amount until maturity including the principal amount. Simply put, coupon bonds are bonds where the issuer makes coupon payments annually or semi-annually and the final amount or face value at maturity date.

PRESENT VALUE OF AN ANNUAL COUPON BOND

The present value or purchase price of an annual coupon bond is the present value of the annual payments plus the present value of the face value. The present value of coupon payment is an annuity.

The formula for present value of an annual coupon bond is given by:

$$P = I \left[\frac{1 - (1 + r)^{-n}}{r} \right] + M (1 + r)^{-n}$$

Where P = present value or purchase price
$\quad$ I = coupon payment in Kwacha
$\quad$ M = face value
$\quad$ r = coupon rate
$\quad$ n = maturity period

Example 4

X Limited issues a 10 year bond with an annual payment of K8 000 000, and similar bonds are offering a rate of 8%. What is the present value of such a bond.

Solution

The first step is for us to determine the face value of this bond using

Coupon payment = coupon rate X face value

K8 000 000 = 0.08M

Face value (M) = K100, 000,000.
r = 0.08
n = 10
I = K8 000 000
P =?

Using $P = I \left[\frac{1 - (1 + r)^{-n}}{r} \right] + M (1 + r)^{-n}$

$\quad = K8\,000\,000 \left[\frac{1 - (1 + 0.08)^{-10}}{0.08} \right] + K100\,000\,000 (1 + 0.08)^{-10}$

$\quad = K8\,000\,000 \; \frac{1 - (1.08)^{-10}}{0.08} + K100\,000\,000 (1.08)^{-10}$

= K8 000 000 (6.710081399) + K100 000 000 (0.463193488)

= K53, 680,651.19 + K46, 319,348.81

= K100, 000,000.

Notes: the present value of coupon payments is calculated using the annuity factor $\left(\dfrac{1 - (1 + r)^{-n}}{r} \right)$ while the present value of the face value is found by the

Discount factor $(1 + r)^{-n}$. Further, the face value of the bond here is equal to its present value. This is always the case where there is only one interest rate (coupon rate) and the bond is traded in an active market. Now, if the present value or purchase price and face value are both K100, 000, 000 how does an investor make profit? Well, certainly the investor makes some profits. The investor will receive K8 000 000 X 10 = K80 000 000 in coupon payments and K100, 000, 000 in face value for a total of K180, 000, 000. Thus, his profit actually is K180, 000,000 - 100 000 000= K80, 000, 000. Clear? I hope so!

PRESENT VALUE OF A SEMI-ANNUAL COUPON BONDS

Generally, bonds pay interest twice a year. The present value or purchase price for a bond that pays interest twice a year is a slight modification to the present value formula for an annual coupon bonds. In particular, we divide coupon payment and coupon rate by two and multiply the periods by two.

A short way to compute this is to recognize that annual coupon payment is paid in two installments (therefore I/2), that coupon rate in half year is half the annual rate (therefore r/2) and finally, periods over which half amounts and half interest are paid twice (therefore 2n).

Thus, the formula becomes:

$$P = I/2 \left(\frac{1 - (1 + r/2)^{-2n}}{r/2} \right) + M (1 + r/2)^{-2n}$$

Where P = present value or purchase price
       I = coupon payment
       r = coupon rate
       n = maturity period
       M = face value

Example 5

X Limited issues a 10 year bond with a face value of K100,000,00 and similar bonds are offering a market rate of 8% compounded semi-annually. What is the present value of such a bond?

Solution

Here M = K100 000 000

$r = \dfrac{8\%}{2} = 4\% = 0.04$

n = 10 X 2 = 20

I = coupon rate X face value ÷ 2

= 0.08 X K100 000 000 ÷ 2

= K8 000 000 ÷ 2

= K4, 000,000.

Using $P = I\left[\dfrac{1-(1+r)^{-n}}{r}\right] + M(1+r)^{-n}$

$= K4\,000\,000\left[\dfrac{1-(1+0.04)^{-20}}{0.04}\right] + K100\,000\,(1+0.04)^{-20}$

$= K4\,000\,000\left[\dfrac{1-(1.04)^{-20}}{0.04}\right] + K100\,000\,000\,(1.04)^{-20}$

= K4 000 000 (13.59032635) + K100 000 000 (0.45638946

= K54, 361,305.40 + K45, 638,694.62

= K100, 000,000

A DETOUR IN BOND COMPUTATIONS

Some bond are said to be bought at a premium or at a discount. A bond is said to be bought at a premium if its purchase price (P) is greater than its face value or redemption value (M). The premium is simply purchase price <u>minus</u> face value.

On the other hand, a bond is said to be bought at a discount if its purchase price (P) is less than its face value (M). The discount is simply face value minus purchase price.

At the basic level, what makes a bond to be said to be bought at a premium or discount is the difference between the bond rate and the yield rate. In the previous examples, the bond rate and the yield rates were the same figure i.e. 8%. If the bond rate is less than the yield rate, we have a discount while if the bond rate is greater than the yield rate, then we have a premium. This is true whether the bond pays interest annually or semi-annually. Have look at the following example.

Example 6

A K5000 000, 3% bond is redeemable at par on July 1, 1990 but may be redeemable on July 1, 1980, or at any interest payment date thereafter.

a) Find the purchase price on July 1, 1963, to yield at least 4% compounded semi-annually.

b) Find the investor's profit if the bond is redeemed on July 1, 1985.

Solution

Since the required rate (yield rate) exceeds the bond rate, the bond must be bought at a discount. The book value of such a bond gradually increases until it reaches the face value on the redemption date. Thus, the investor must compute his price under the assumption that the bond will be redeemed at the latest possible date.

The purchase price is the present value of the bond and is calculated using the following formula:

$$P = I \left[\frac{1 - (1 + r)^{-n}}{r} \right] + M (1 + r)^{-n}$$

Where P = purchase price
I = coupon payment in Kwacha
M = face value (redemption value)
r = coupon rate

$$\left(\frac{1 - (1 + r)^{-n}}{r} \right) = \text{annuity factor}$$

$$(1 + r)^{-n} = \text{discount factor}$$

Since compounding is semi-annual, we divide the yield rate, by 2 and multiply the number of periods, n, by 2.

Thus, $r = \frac{4\%}{2} = 2$

n = 1990 – 1963 = 27 years; 27 X 2 = 54
M = K5000 000 as given
I = K75 000

Using the purchase price (present value) formula of a bond and substituting, we have

$$P_o = K75\ 000 \frac{(1 - (1.02)^{-54}}{0.02} + K5000\ 000\ (1.02)^{-54}$$

= K75 000 (32.83828327) + K5000 000 (0.34 3234334)

= K2, 462,871.245 + K1, 716,171.673

= K4, 179,042.918

= <u>K4, 179,042.92</u>

c) By 1985, the book value of the bond will have increased to the purchase price on that date to yield 4% compounded semi-annually.

r = $\frac{4\%}{2}$ = 2% = 0.02

n = 1990 – 1985 = 5 years: 5 X 2 = 10 years.

M = K5000 000

I = K75 000

Thus, K75 000 $\left[\dfrac{1-(1.02)^{-10}}{0.02}\right]$ + K5000 000 $(1.02)^{-10}$

= K75 000 (8.982585006) + K5000 000 (0.8203448299)

= K673, 693 8755 + K4, 101,741.495

= K40, 775, 435.371

Thus, profit is K5000 000 – K4, 775,435.37

K224, 564.63

CALCULATING THE YIELD RATE 2

Tables are normally used to determine the yield rates. However, here we attempt to determine the yield rate by computation. Particularly, we employ the interpolation method.

The interpolation method requires the purchase price of the bond for two interest rates such that one price is smaller and the other is greater than the given quoted price. Since this is an estimate we, can improve our accuracy by narrowing the limits of rates chosen. Let's now take a look at the above technique by way of an example.

Example 7

A K10 000 000, 3% bond redeemable at par on July 1, 2007 is bought for K9, 525,000 on July 1, 1993. Find the yield rate, compounded semi-annually.

Solution

Since on July 1, 1993 the purchase price to yield 3% compounded annually is K10 000 000, the actual yield rate is larger. The price to yield, say, 3.5% compounded semi annually is:

Here M = K10 000 000

r = $\frac{3.5\%}{2}$ = 1.75% = 0.175

n = 2007 – 1993 = 14 X 2 = 28

I = 0.03 X K10 000 00 ÷ 2 = K150, 000

Using P = I $\left[\dfrac{1-(1+r)^{-n}}{r}\right]$ + $(1+r)^{-n}$

$$= K150\ 000 \left[\frac{1 - (1 + 0.0175)^{-28}}{0.0175} \right] + K10\ 000\ 000\ (1 + 0.0175)^{-28}$$

$$= K150\ 000 \left[\frac{1 - (1.0175)^{-28}}{0.0175} \right] + K10\ 000\ 000\ (1.0175)^{-28}$$

$$= K150\ (21.98695474) - K10\ 000\ 000\ (0.615228292)$$

$$= K3,\ 298,043.211 + K6,\ 152,282.92$$

$$= K9,\ 450,326.131$$

$$= \underline{K9,\ 450,326.13}$$

Thus, the yield is between 3% and 3.5% compounded semi-annually. To estimate the yield rate, we set our work as follows:

$$0.0025 \begin{bmatrix} 0.015 \\ r \\ 0.0175 \end{bmatrix} \quad x \qquad {}^{-}549,673.87 \quad \begin{bmatrix} 10\ 000\ 000.00 \\ 9\ 525\ 000.00 \\ 9\ 450\ 326.13 \end{bmatrix} {}^{-}475\ 000$$

Then we solve for x in the above setting as follows:

$$x = \frac{475\ 000}{549\ 673.87} \quad X\ 0.0025$$

$$= 0.86414877\ X\ 0.0025$$

$$= 0.002160371931$$

$$= 0.00216$$

Then r = 0.015 + 0.00216 = 0.01716 = 0.01716 x 2 = 3.432%

Hence the yield rate is 3.432% compounded semi-annually.

Notes: The following should be noted from the above computation.

1. 0.015 is the 3% divided by 2 (i.e. semi-annual).
2. 0.0175 is the 3.5% divided by 2
3. 0.0025 = 0.015 – 0.0175
4. K549 673.87 = K10 000 000 – K9 450 326.13
5. K375 000 = K10 000 000 – K9 525 000
6. To solve for x and r in the above set up, we need to simply grasp the way figures are picked up. Otherwise, we can form simultaneous equations and then use matrix algebra to solve for x and r. However, matrix algebra is beyond the task of this book.

Alternatively, we can determine the interest rate on a bond held to maturity by using the approximate formula as follows:

$$YTM = \frac{I + \dfrac{(M - p)}{N}}{\dfrac{2p + M}{3}}$$

Where M = face value
P = Purchase price
N = Maturity period
I = Coupon payment
YTM = Yield to maturity

Thus, $YTM = \dfrac{150\ 000 + \dfrac{(10\ 000\ 000 - 9525\ 000)}{28}}{\dfrac{2(9525\ 000) + 10\ 000\ 000}{3}}$

$$= \frac{150\ 000 + 16964.28571}{9683\ 333.333}$$

$$= \frac{166\ 964.2857}{9683\ 333.\ 333}$$

$$= 0.017242439 \times 100 = 1.7242439\%$$

Since compounding is semi- annually, we multiply by 2 i.e. 1.7242439% x 2 = 3.4484878% = 3.45% which is closer to one calculated earlier.

Similarly, the yield to maturity for callable bonds can be determined in much the same way as for non-callable bonds. To call a bond or to redeem a bond is to buy back from the investor according to stated conditions in the bond indenture (bond contract).

Thus,
$$YTC = \frac{I + \dfrac{(C - P)}{N}}{\dfrac{2P + C}{3}}$$

Where I = Coupon payment
C = Call price
P = Purchase price
N = Maturity period
YTC = Yield to call

BOND SCHEDULE

A bond schedule is simply a table that shows the state of the bond at any given period.

The bond schedule normally shows the following for each period:

b)   Book value of the bond at the beginning of the period

c)   Interest due on the book value
d)   Bond interest payment (coupon payment)
e)   Change in the book value

The bond value of a bond at any given period is the sum invested in the bond at that time. The value of a bond on the date of purchase is the purchase price while the book value on the redemption date is the redemption value (face value). The change in the book value over the life of a bond is best shown by constructing an investment schedule as illustrated by, the next example.

Example 8

A K100 000 00 8% bond redeemable at par on January 1, 2007 is bought on July 1, 2004 to yield 10% compounded semi-annually. Construct an investment schedule.

Solution

If an investor purchases a bond on an interest payment date, he buys the right to receive certain future payments. However, he does not receive the interest payment due on the date of purchase.

In the given question, the number of periods is 5 i.e. 2½ years multiplied by 2 since compounding is semi-annually.

Thus, M = K100 000 000

$$r_1 = \frac{8\%}{2} = 4\% = 0.04$$

$$r_2 = \frac{10\%}{2} = 5\% = 0.05$$

$$n = 2\tfrac{1}{2} \times 2 = 5$$

$$I = 0.04 \times K100\,000\,000 = K4\,000\,000$$

Using $P = I \left[\frac{1 - (1 + r)^{-n}}{r} \right] + M(1 + r)^{-n}$

$$= K4000\,000 \left[\frac{1 - (1 + 0.05)^{-5}}{0.05} \right] + K100\,000\,000\,(1 + 0.05)^{-5}$$

$$= K4000\,000 \left[\frac{1 - (1.05)^{-5}}{0.05} \right] + K100\,000\,000\,(1.05)^{-5}$$

$$= K4000\,000\,(4.329476671) + K100\,000\,000\,(0.783526166)$$

$$= K17,317,906.68 + K78,352,616.65$$

$$= K95,670523.63 \text{ i.e. book value at July, 2004}$$

Now you may have been wondering as to why we have two interest rates. Well, they are needed to complete the investment schedule.

Period	Book value at Beginning of period	interest due on book value	Bond interest payment	Change in book value
1	95, 670523.63	4, 783,526.382	4 000 000	783,526.3315
2	96, 454,052.96	4, 822,702.648	4 000 000	822,702.6481
3	97, 276,755.61	4, 863,837.78	4 000 000	863,837.7804
4	98, 140,593.39	4,907,029.67	4 000 000	907,029.6695
5	99,047,632.06	4,952,381.153	4 000 000	952,381.153
6	100, 000,004.2	-	-	-

Notes to calculations:

1. The book value at the beginning of any period price at which the bond must be bought to yield the investor's rate.

2. Interest due = 5% of book value at beginning of period.

3. Interest payment = 4% of the face value.

4. Change in book value = interest due less interest payment

5. Book value at beginning (New) = to book value at beginning (previous period) Plus change in book value.

6. You need to find the best quick way of completing the schedule by immediately using the figures from the calculator to reduce number punching!

7. Above bond was bought at a discount. When a bond is bought at a premium, we amortize the principal to bring it down to redemption value. The principals are similar.

Example 9

Construct an investment schedule for a K100 000 000, 10% bond redeemable on January 1, 2007 bought on July 1, 2004 to yield 8% compounded semi-annually.

Solution

Here n = 2½ years X 2 = 5

$$r_1 = \frac{10\%}{2} = 5\% = 0.05$$

$$r_2 = \frac{8\%}{2} = 4\% = 0.04$$

Cryford Mumba

$$I = 0.05 \times K100\ 000\ 000 = K5\ 000\ 000$$

$$M = K100\ 000\ 000$$

Using $P = I\left[\dfrac{1-(1+r)^{-n}}{R}\right] + M(1+r)^{-n}$

$$= K5000\ 000\left[\dfrac{1-(1+0.04)^{-5}}{0.04}\right] + K100\ 000\ 000(1+0.04)^{-5}$$

$$= K5000\ 000\ (4.45\ 1822331) + K100\ 000\ 000\ (0.821927106)$$

$$= K22,259,111.65 + K82,192\ 710.68$$

$$= \underline{K104,\ 451,822.30}$$

The book value on the date of purchase is K104, 451, 822.30 hence the bond is bought at a premium. The schedule is as follows:

Period	Book value at beginning of period	Interest due on book value	Bond interest payment	Change in book value
1	104, 451,822.30	4,178,072.892	5000 000	821, 927.108
2	103, 629,895.20	4,145,195.808	5000 000	854,804.1923
3	102, 775,091.00	4,111,003.64	5000 000	888,996.3597
4	101, 886,094.60	4,075,443.786	5000 000	924,556.2144
5	100, 961,538.40	4,038,461.535	5000 000	961,538.465
6	99, 999,999.94	-	-	-

Notes to calculations

1. The book value at the beginning of any period is the price at which the bond must be bought to yield the investor's rate.

2. Interest due = 4% of book value at beginning of period.

3. Interest payment = 5% of face value

4. Change in book value = interest payment less interest due. Thus, change in book value represents repayments of capital since we have a bond at a premium.

5. New book value at the beginning of period = book value at beginning (previous period) less change in book value

6. Book value at the beginning of period 6 should have been K100 000 000 but is less due to rounding off of figures.

Learn and understand the above two examples.

166

SERIAL BONDS

Serial bonds are simply several distinct bonds combined under one contract. To find the present value or purchase value of serial bonds, all we need to do is to compute the present value of each payment and then sum them as illustrated by the example below:

Example 10

A serial bond issue of K100 000 000 with interest at 10% compounded semi-annually is to be redeemed by payments of K50 000 000 in 10 years, K50 000 000 in 12 years and K100 000 000 in 15 years. Find the purchase price of the issue to yield 8% compounded semi-annually.

Solution

The above serial bond is equivalent to three ordinary bonds, one with a face value of K50 000 000 redeemable at par in 10 years, another with a face value of K50 000 000 redeemable at par in 12 years, and one with the face value of K100 000 000 redeemable at par in 15 years. The required purchase price is the sum of the prices of the three bonds to yield 8% compounded semi-annually.

Thus, using $P = I \left[\dfrac{1 - (1 + r)^{-n}}{r} \right] + M (1 + r)^{-n}$

For K50 000 000 bond redeemable in 10 years

$I = 0.05 \times K50\ 000\ 000 = K2,500,000$
$M = K50\ 000\ 000$
$r = 0.04,$
$n = 20$

For K50 000 000 bond redeemable in 12 years

$I = 0.05 \times K50\ 000\ 000 = K2,500,000$

$M = K50\ 000\ 000$
$r = 0.04$
$n = 24$

For K100 000 000 bond redeemable in 15 years

$I = 0.05 \times K100\ 000\ 000 = K5,000\ 000$
$M = K100\ 000\ 000$
$r = 0.04$
$n = 30$

Using above information, we have

$P = K2,500,000 \left[\dfrac{1 - 1.04)^{-20}}{0.04} \right] + K50\ 000\ 000\ (1.04)^{-20}$

$+ K2,500,000 \left[\dfrac{1 - (1.04)^{-24}}{0.04} \right] + K50\ 000\ 000\ (1.04)^{-24}$

$$+ \text{K}5000\,000 \left[\frac{1 - (1.04)^{-30}}{0.04} \right] + \text{K}50\,000\,000\,(1.04)^{-30}$$

$$= \text{K}2\,500\,000\,(13.59032635) + \text{K}50\,000\,000\,(0.456386946)$$

$$+ \text{K}2\,500\,000\,(15.2496314) + \text{K}50\,000\,000\,(0.390121474)$$

$$+ \text{K}5000\,000\,(17.2920333) + \text{K}100\,000\,000\,(0.308318668)$$

$$= \text{K}33,\,975,815.88 + \text{K}22,\,819,347.30 + \text{K}38,\,124,078.50$$

$$+ \text{K}19,\,506,\,073.70 + \text{K}86,\,460,166.50 + \text{K}30,\,831,866.80$$

$$= \underline{\text{K}231,\,717,348.70}$$

The purchase price is K231, 717,348.70 which is greater than K200 000 000 face value hence the serial bond issue is at a premium. Remember a bond is issued at a premium if the yield rate is greater than the bond rate. Or put simply when the purchase price is greater than the face value of a bond.

ADDENDUM: TREASURY BILL PRICING MECHANISM

A treasury bill is a short term paper issued by the government of the republic of Zambia. It obliges the government to pay the holder or bearer a fixed sum of money after a specified number of days from the date of issue. The days usually are 91 days, 182 days, 283 days etc

The bank of Zambia applies the multiple price system to price treasury bills. This means that each successful bidder is allocated treasury bills are sold at a discount. The return to the investor is the difference between the purchase price and the face or par value.

(d) Discount rate - This is the discount amount divided by the face value expressed as a percentage annualized using a 365 day-year.

> Discount rate $= \dfrac{(F - P)}{F} \times \dfrac{D}{n} \times 100$

Where D = Number of days in a year (365)
> F = face value
> P = purchase (cost) price
> N = Maturity period of investment.

(e) The yield rate – This is the rate of return on the cost of treasury bills invested. It is obtained as a discount amount divided by the cost of the treasury bill expressed as a percentage annualized on a 365 day-year.

> Yield rate $\dfrac{(F - P)}{P} \times \dfrac{D}{n} \times 100$

Where F = face value
   P = purchase (cost) price
   D = Number of days in a year (365)
   N = Maturity period of investment

Example 10

A treasury bill with a face value of K100 000 000 is issued at K9 670 000 for 28 days. Find:

(a)   Discount rate
(b)   Yield rate

Solution

(a) Discount rate = $\frac{(F - P)}{F} \times \frac{D}{n} \times 100$

   F = K100 000 000
   P = K96 670 000
   D = 365 days
   n = 28 days

= $\frac{(100\ 000\ 000 - 96\ 670\ 000)}{100\ 000\ 000} \times \frac{365}{28} \times 100$

   = 0.0333 x 13.03571429 x 100

   = 43.4089285%

   = 43.4%

(b) Yield rate = $\frac{(F - P)}{P} \times \frac{D}{n} \times 100$

   F = K100 000 000
   P = K96 670 000
   D = 365 days
   n = 28 days

= $\frac{(100\ 000\ 000 - 96\ 670\ 000)}{96\ 670\ 000} \times \frac{365}{28} \times 100$

   = 0.034447088 x 13.03571429 x 100

   = 44.9042397%

   = 44.9%

Example 11

PCBF Ltd bids 1125175.85 for a 91 – day K100 000 000 treasury bill. If the bid is accepted, what yield will PCBF get on?

(f) a bank discount basis?
(g) a simple interest basis?

Solution

Firstly, we need to determine the purchase price by subtracting the bid from the face value.

Thus, K100 000 000 – K1125175.85 = K98, 874,824.15

F = K100 000 000
P = K98 874 824.15
D = 365 days
n = 91 days

(a) Bank discount basis = $\dfrac{F-P}{F}$ x $\dfrac{D}{n}$ x 100

$$= \frac{K100\,000\,000 - K98874824.15}{K100\,000\,000} \times \frac{365}{91} \times 100$$

$$= 0.011251758 \times 4.010989011 \times 100$$

$$= 4.5130667\%$$

$$= 4.51\%$$

(b) Simple interest basis, yield = $\dfrac{F-P}{P}$ x $\dfrac{D}{n}$ x 100

$$= \frac{K100\,000\,000 - K198\,874\,824.15}{K98\,874\,824.15} \times \frac{365}{91} \times 100$$

$$= 0.011379801 \times 4.010989011 \times 100$$

$$= 4.564425\%$$

$$= 4.56\%$$

PROGRESS CLINIC 9

1. Find the annuity for a GRZ coupon bond issued for the face value of K30 000 000 redeemable in 8 years at 12% rate compounded annually.

2. Find the annuity for a GRZ coupon bond issued for the face value of K30 000 000 redeemable in 8years at 12% rate compounded semi-annually.

3. What is the purchase price of a GRZ pure bond issued for 8 years with a face value of K30 000 000, if the investor requires a yield of 15% per annum.

4. PCBF Limited has issued a 10 year corporate bond with an annual payment of K10 000 000 and similar bonds are offering at a rate of 5% per annum. The company wants to utilize the funds so raised to facilitate its expansion..

   a) Find the maturity value of the bond issued by PCBF Limited

   b) Find the present value of the corporate bond above.

5. PCBF Limited has issued another corporate bond which matures in 10 years with a face value of K200 000 000 and similar bonds are offering a market rate of 5% compounded semi-annually. What is the present value of such a bond?

6. A K65 000 000, 10% is redeemable at par on January 1, 2020, but may be redeemable on January 1, 2010 or at any interest payment date thereafter.

   a. Find the purchase price on January 1, 1993 to yield at least 15% compounded semi-annually.

   b. Find the investor's profit if the bond is redeemed on January 1, 2015.

7. Construct an investment schedule for a K30 000 000, 12% bond redeemable on December 31, 2010 bought on June 30, 2007, to yield 9% compounded semi-annually.

8. A K30 000 000, 9% bond redeemable at par on December 31, 2010 is bought on June 30, 2007 to yield 12% compounded semi-annually. Construct an investment schedule.

9. A serial bond issue of K100 000 000 with interest at 5% compounded semi annually is to be redeemed by payments of K25 000 000 in 5 years, K25 000 000 in 6 years and K50 000 000 in 9 years. Find the purchase price of the issue to yield 3% compounded semi-annually.

CHAPTER 10

EXPECTATIONS AND MORTALITIES

INTRODUCTION

To calculate life insurance premiums, the size of annuity payments which are made so long as the person is alive, retirement pensions and other related issues, it is essential to know something about the probabilities that a person will stay alive for a given length of time. Actuaries base these probabilities on various kinds of mortality tables which report such things as death for any age, life expectancy for any age or the number of persons still alive at any given age. Most of the mortality tables used today are based on several experiences among lives insured by several large American Insurance Companies and they are revised continuously in line with medical advance, changes in living conditions, health standards and so on.

In this chapter we centre our discussion on expectations, life annuities and endowments.

EXPECTATIONS

An expected value (EV) is a weighted average value based on probability. The expected value for a single event can offer a helpful guide for management decisions. Probability is defined as the livelihood or chance of something happening. There are two common ways of calculating probability depending on whether some experiment is performed or not.

> a. Theoretical probability is the name given to probability that is calculated without the experiment being performed, that is using only information that is known about the physical situations e.g. the probability of it raining today!
>
> b. Empirical or statistical probability is the name given to probability that is calculated using the results of an experiment that has been performed a number of times. Note that empirical probability is also known as relative frequency or subjective probability.

The following are the common probability results:

a) probability of 1 indicates certainty
b) probability of 0 indicates impossibility
c) probability of 0.5 indicates 50% chance
d) Probability limits are in the range 0 to 1.
e) Complementary probability $P(A) = 1 - P(A)$.

More detailed discussion on probability computations are reserved for BF 260 Statistical Analysis.

DECISION CRITERIA: EXPECTED VALUES

The following highlights the decision criteria using the expected value technique:

a) If a project has a positive expected value, then it should be accepted.
b) If a project has a negative expected value, then it should be rejected.
c) If two or more projects are being compared, the one with the highest positive expected value is preferred.

CALCULATION OF EXPECTED VALUE

The expected value is calculated using the following formula:

$$EV = \sum xP(x)$$

Where $\sum$ = summation
  EV = expected value
  x = random variable
  P(x) = probability of the random variable

Example 1

The daily sales of product T is as follows

Units	Probability
1000	0.2
2000	0.3
3000	0.4
4000	0.1
	1.0

Calculate the expected daily sales of product T.

Solution

Units (x)	Probability (P (x)	xP(x)
1000	0.2	200
2000	0.3	600
3000	0.4	1200
4000	0.1	400
		2400 units

Using the formula given above:

$$EV = \sum xP(x)$$

$$= 1000 (0.2) + 2000 (0.3) + 3000 (0.4) + 4000 (0.1)$$

$$= 200 + 600 + 1200 + 400$$

$$= \underline{2400 \text{ units}}$$

So the expected daily sales is 2400 units which is also the mean of the random variable x.

Note that mean $(\bar{x})$ = $\dfrac{\sum x}{n}$

$$= \dfrac{1000 + 2000 + 3000 + 4000}{4}$$

$$= \dfrac{10\ 000}{4}$$

$$= \underline{2500\ units}$$

The expected value as a weighted average must always be within the given range of values and not outside. In the above example, the range is from 1000 to 4000 units.

Example 2

A bank is opening a new branch and two sites are available to it. These sites are A and B. From past experience, the bank calculates that the probability of success on site A is 0.8 with annual profit of K500 000 000. If not successful annual loss is estimated at K80 000 000. For site B, the corresponding figures are 0.6 for success with annual profit of K600 000 000 or an annual loss of K120 000 000.

Where should the branch be located in order to maximize profits

Solution

Profit = Total revenue – Total costs.

Hence we need to calculate the EV for each site.

For site A,

Profit = K500 000 000 with a probability of 0.8

Loss = K80 000 000 with a probability of 0.2 (i.e. 1 - 0.8)

EV = K500 000 000 (0.8) – K80 000 000 (0.2)

= K400 000 0000 – K16 000 000

= K384 000 000

For site B:

Profit = K600 000 000 with probability of 0.6

Loss = K120 000 000 with probability of 0.4 (i.e. 1 – 0.6)

EV = K600 000 000 (0.6) – K120 000 000 (0.4)

= K360 000 000 – K48 000 000

= K312 000 000

The expected value on site A is greater by K72 000 000 hence the branch should be located at site A

EXPECTATIONS AND FUTURE VALUES

Expectation in simple terms is the product of the random variable x multiplied by the probability of the random variable x. To simplify our computations, we will denote the probability of random variable x as simply P © PCBF 2008

and the random variable x as S. Using this new notation, expectation can be calculated as:

Expectation = PS

At times, it is not enough to simply compute expectation but to find the present value of that expectation. Put is differently, an investor may wish to know the present value of the future sum i.e. how much should be invested not to equal a certain sum in future.

The present value of an expected n is calculated using the following formula:

$$\text{Present value of expectation} = (1 + r)^{-n} PS \text{ or } PS (1 + r)^{-n}$$

Where r = interest rate
P = probability
S = future value
PS = expectation
$(1 + r)^{-n}$ = discount factor

Example 3

From past experience, Premier College management estimates that he probability that a student will complete the Diploma in Banking and finance within 2years is 0.7. John has been promised a promotion to the rank of Branch Manager where he will pocket K15 000 000 net upon program completion 2 years from today.

If money is worth 6%, find:

a) his expectation
b) present value of his expectation

Solution

a)   Expectation is given by PS

Here P = 0.7
S = K15 000 000

Hence, his expectation = 0.7 (15 000 000) = <u>K10, 500,000</u>

b)   Present value of his expectation is given by:

$(1 + r)^{-n} PS$

Where n = 2 years
    r = 0.06
    PS = expectation

Thus, present value of his expectation is:

$= (1 + 0.06)^{-2} 10, 500,000$

$= (1.06)^{-2} 10\ 500\ 000$

= 0.8899644 X 10, 500,000

= <u>K9, 344,962.62</u>

Thus, the present value of his expectation is K9, 344,962.62

MORTALITY TABLES

A mortality table is simply a summary of the life records of a large representative group of individuals i.e. death, life expectancies, living at a given age, and so on. There are various mortality tables but the principles behind them all are similar. The most common of these is the American Experience Table of mortality first published in 1868 and which has since been replaced by the CSO table. In this section, we will use the CSO table

From the table, the following should be clear:

a)   The table has seven columns, with the first and the last column being similar. This is done to aid quick access to figures within the table. The ages range from 0 to 99 years.

A brief explanation of the columns is as follows:

1.   Column 1 and 7 – These two columns are concerned with AGE. The age we can predict how many persons limit is 0 to 99. From this are still alive, dying and son on. An individual's age denoted by x, which means that the original group of $L0 = 1,023102$

2.   Individuals of which $L1 = 1,000,000$ were alive at age 1 while do = 23102 died at 0. The table assumes that no individual will attain 100 years.

3. Column 2 – This gives the number of persons living at any given age x I.e. number living Lx e.g. L40 = 883 342 implying that 883 342 are still alive at age 40.

4. Column 3 – this column gives the number of deaths within the year from age x to age x + 1. It is headed dx i.e. dying at age x. Note that dx = Lx – Lx + 1 denotes number of people aged x dying within 1 year while dx = Lx – Lx + n denotes number of people aged x dying after n years.

5. Column 4 and 5 (Nx and Dx) are used for life annuities

6. Column 6 Mx is used for life insurance policies.

GENERAL MORTALITY RULES

Rule 1: In general, the probability that a person aged x will still be alive at age n is given by the ratio $\dfrac{Lx + n}{Lx}$

Example 4

Find the probability that a person aged 40 will still be alive at 65.

Solution

Lx = 40, Lx + n = 65.

Thus,

$$\frac{L65}{L40} = \frac{577882}{883\ 342}$$

$$= 0.654199619$$

$$= \underline{0.6542}$$

Rule 2: In general, the probability that a person aged x will die within a year is given by the ratio $\dfrac{Lx - Lx + 1}{Lx}$

Example 5

Find the probability that a person aged 54 will die within a year

Solution

The probability is the ratio of the number of persons alive at age 54 minus the number of persons alive at age 55 to the number of persons alive at age 54.

Thus,

$$\frac{L54 - L55}{L54} = \frac{766961 - 754191}{766961}$$

$$= 0.016650129$$

$$= \underline{0.167}$$

Rule 3: In general, the probability that a person aged x will no longer be alive
at age n is given by the ratio:

$$\frac{Lx - Lx + n}{Lx}$$

Example 6

What is the probability that a person aged 20 will no longer be alive at age 35?

Solution

Lx = 20, Lx + n = 35

Using

$$\frac{Lx - Lx + n}{Lx} = \frac{L20 - L35}{L20}$$

$$= \frac{951\,483 - 906\,554}{951\,483}$$

$$= \frac{44929}{951483}$$

$$= 0.047219971$$

$$= \underline{0.0472}$$

Rule 4: In general, the probability that a person aged x will be alive at age n
but die before age z reaching age z is given by the ratio.

$$\frac{Lx + n - Lz}{Lx}$$

Example 7

Find the probability that a person aged 25 will be alive at age 50 but die before
reaching 60.

Solution

Lx = 25, Lx + n = 50, Lz = 60

Using

$$\frac{Lx + n - Lz}{Lx} = \frac{L50 - L60}{L25}$$

$$= \frac{810\,900 - 677\,771}{939\,197}$$

$$= \frac{133\,129}{939\,197}$$

$$= 0.141747684$$

$$= \underline{0.1417}$$

ALTERNATIVE APPROACH TO ABOVE RULES

The following approach can be taken as an alternative to rules given above but with same results.

i. P_x – This is the probability that a person aged x will live at least one year i.e. will attain x + 1.

Example 8

Find the probability that a person aged 54 will live for at least one year.
Solution

$$P_{20} = \frac{L55}{L54} = \frac{754191}{766961}$$

$$= 0.98334987$$

$$= \underline{0.9833}$$

ii. $_nP_x$ – This is the probability than a person aged x will live for at least n years, i.e. will attain age x + n.

Example 9

Find the probability that a person aged 40 will attain the age 65.

Solution

We want to find the probability of a person aged 40 to live for at least 25 years.

$$_{25}P_{40} = \frac{L65}{L40} = \frac{577\,882}{883\,342}$$

$$= 0.654199619$$

$$= 0.6542$$

iii. q_x – This is the probability that a person aged x will not live a full year, i.e. will not attain age x + 1.

Example 10

Find the probability that a person aged 54 will not live a full year i.e. will not attain age 55.

Solution

Here dx = d54 = 12 770

$$Lx = L54 = 766\ 961$$

Using

$$\frac{dx}{Lx} = \frac{d54}{L54} = \frac{12\ 770}{766\ 961}$$

$$= 0.016650129$$

$$= \underline{0.0167}$$

Note that this is the same solution we found using Rule 2. Since both can give the same solution, you can choose which one you are more comfortable with and use it!

iv. $_n q_x$ – This is the probability that a person aged x will not live for n years, i.e. will not attain age x + n.

Example 11

Find the probability that a person aged 20 will die before attaining 35.

Solution

We want to find the probability that a person aged 25 will not live for the next 35 – 20 = 15 years

Hence,

$$_{15} P_{20} = \frac{L20 - L35}{L20} = \frac{951\ 483 - 906\ 554}{951\ 483}$$

$$= \frac{44\ 929}{951\ 483}$$

$$= 0.047219971$$

$$= \underline{0.0472}$$

APPLICATIONS OF MORTALITY TABLES AND EXPECTATION PRINCIPLES

One of the most important developments of recent years has been the increasing role played by mathematics in decision making on the managerial

level. We cannot judge what is probable unless we know what is possible, but to make intelligent decisions, even though that is not enough – we must also know something about the consequences (profits, losses, gains, penalties or rewards) of everything that can possibly take place.

Originally, the concept of mathematical expectation arose in connection with games of chance, and in its simplest form it is the product of the probability that a player will win and the amount he stands to win and mortalities in connection with the cost of a pure endowment and life annuities

COST OF A PURE ENDOWMENT

The cost of a pure endowment is a typical example of a mathematical expectation. It is an insurance policy which will pay a person a specified sum of money after a given number of years *provided he is still alive to receive it*. Of paramount importance to pure endowment computations is the knowledge of the age of a person now (x) and the age when he is expected to receive the money (x + n), as well as money's worth i.e. interest rate.

Earlier, we computed expectation using PS and the present value of that expectation using $(1 + r)^{-n}$ PS. Now taking P the probability of a person aged x to attain age x + n, this probability can be presented as:

$$_n p_x = \frac{Lx + n}{Lx}$$

Taking S to be k1, the expectation will be

$$\frac{Lx + n}{Lx} \quad (1)$$

Hence the present value of the expectation ($_n E_x$) is given by the following formula

$$_n E_x = (1 + r)^{-n} \frac{Lx + n}{Lx}$$

Where x = person's age now
        n = Age when receiving endowment minus age now.

    Lx = Number of people alive at age x
    Lx + n = Number of people alive at age x + n
    $_n E_x$ = expectation present value.
    r = Interest rate (i.e. money's worth).

Example 12

On his 35th birthday, Mark uses K25 million of his savings to purchase a pure endowment payable if and when he attains age 65. Assuming that he survives, how much will he receive on 3.5% basis? What is the present value of the endowment?

Solution

Here x = 35, n = 65 – 35 = 30, r = 0.035, Lx + n = 65, Lx = 35

Using

$$_nE_x = (1 + r)^{-n} \frac{Lx + n}{Lx}$$

$$K25\ 000\ 000\ _{30}E_{35} = K25\ 000\ 000\ (1 + 0.035)^{-30} \frac{L65}{L35}$$

$$= K25\ 000\ 000\ (1.035)^{-30} \frac{577\ 882}{906\ 554}$$

$$= K25\ 000\ 000 \times 0.35627841 \times 0.637449065$$

$$= K5,677,733.487$$

$$= \underline{K5,677,733.49}\ \text{This is the present value of the endowment.}$$

Now the net premium for an endowment of K1 is $_{30}E_{35} = (1.035)^{-30} \frac{L65}{L35}$

With K25 000 000 Mark will be able to purchase an endowment of:

$$\frac{K25\ 000\ 000}{_{30}E_{35}} = K25\ 000\ 000\ (1.035)^{+30} \frac{L35}{L65}$$

$$= K25\ 000\ 000 \times 2.806793705 \times \frac{906\ 554}{577\ 882}$$

$$= K25\ 000\ 000 \times 2.806793705 \times 1.56875279$$

$$= \underline{K110,079,136.40}$$

Note: the above computation provides rich insights regarding the treatment of n and the probability $\frac{Lx + n}{Lx}$ when we want to compute the present value of an endowment and when we receive. In the first instance, we want to determine how much one should invest now to receive a specified sum in future (present value or purchase price) while in the later we want to find the terminal value. Thus, for present value we used $(1.035)^{-35} \frac{L65}{L35}$ but for terminal value we used $(1.035)^{-30} \frac{L35}{L65}$. It is all about changing the subject from the discount formula to the compounding one! Hope it is very clear!

ADDENDUM

If the compounding is done for a period less than one year, the single net premium a person of age x has to pay for a pure endowment paying a Kwacha after n years is given by:

$$A\left(\frac{1 + r}{m}\right)^{-mn} \left(\frac{Lx + n}{Lx}\right)$$

Where r = interest rate

m = frequency of compounding a year

LIFE ANNUITIES

Another important application of the formula for mathematical expectation arise in connection with life annuities, such as pension payments which are made for a certain period of time or so long as the person is alive.

By definition, a life annuity is an annuity whose payments continue for all or for some portion of the life of the annuitant i.e. the person who makes payments. These payments may be made annually, semi-annually, quarterly, monthly or weekly. Our discussion here will be limited to annually payments type only.

TYPES OF LIFE ANNUITIES

There are two main types of life annuities namely temporarily life annuities and whole life annuities. The may additionally be deferred or immediate.

- *Deferred temporarily life annuity* – this is a life annuity which ends after a specified number of payments even though the annuitant is still alive. It is "temporary" because there are no payments after a fixed number of years, "deferred" because there are no payments until the end of the year and "life" because each payment is contingent upon the recipient's still being alive.

- If a life annuity is not deferred, it is referred to as *immediate* or *ordinary*, and if payments continue so long as the recipient is alive, it is referred to as a whole life annuity. Thus, a *whole life annuity* is an annuity whose payments continue as long as the annuitant or ordinary depending on when payment has to start i.e. at the beginning (whole life annuity due) or at the end of the year ordinary whole life annuity). The same applies to temporary life annuities.

  The net single payment or required annual payment or present value of an ordinary whole life annuity is calculated using the following formula:

$$R \; \frac{Nx + 1}{Dx} = \text{Net single premium}$$

  Where R = required annual payment

  Nx + 1 = age of a person when the first payment is due

  Dx = age of a person when annuity is taken.

Example 13

John receives K300 000 000 from a retirement fund when he is aged 58. What annual payments will he receive if he uses this sum?

a)   an ordinary whole life annuity

b)   a whole life whose first payment will be at age 66.

Solution

a)   An ordinary whole life annuity commences at the end of the payment period.

Here Total Amount = K300 000 000

$$N_y = N59$$
$$Dx = D58$$

Using

$$R \frac{Nx}{Dx} = \text{Total amount}$$

We have $R \frac{N59}{D58} = K300\,000\,000$

Making R the subject of the formula:

$$R = K300\,000\,000 \times \frac{D58}{N59}$$

From whole life annuity tables i.e. columns 4 and 5

$D_{58} = 169777.17$

$N_{59} = 2027488.15$

Thus, $R = K300\,000\,000 \times \frac{169777.17}{2027488.15}$

$= K300\,000\,000 \times 0.08337687$

$= \underline{K25,\,121,\,306.38}$

b) Here first payment is due at the age of 66, hence N_{66}

Thus using the same formula:

$$R = \frac{N66}{D58} = K300\,000\,000$$

Making R the subject of the formula:

$$R = K300\,000\,000 \times \frac{D58}{N66}$$

Form tables in columns 4 and 5

$D58 = 169777.17$
$N66 = 1056041.64$

$R = K300\,000\,000 \times \underline{169777.17}$

$$1056041.64$$

$$= K300\ 000\ 000 \times 0.160767495$$

$$= \underline{K48,\ 230,248.76}$$

Example 14

Find the net single premium for an ordinary whole life annuity of K10 000 000 per year for a person currently aged 45.

Solution

Here R = K10 000 000
$$N_x = N_{46}$$
$$D_x = D_{45}$$

Using $R = \dfrac{N_x}{D_x}$ = Net Single Premium

$$K10\ 000\ 000 \times \frac{N_{46}}{D_{45}} = \text{Net Single Premium}$$

$$K10\ 000\ 000 \times \frac{4,\ 881,357.05}{280,\ 638.95}$$

$$K10\ 000\ 000 \times 17.39372617$$

$$\underline{K173,\ 937,261.70}$$

Example 15

Find the net single premium for a whole life annuity due of K10 000 000 per year for a person currently aged 45.

Solution

Here $N_x = N_{45}$
$$D_x = D_{45}$$

Using $R\ \dfrac{N_x}{D_x}$ = Net Single Premium

$$K10\ 000\ 000 \times \frac{N_{45}}{D_{45}} = \text{Net Single Premium}$$

$$= K10\ 000\ 000 \times \frac{5,\ 161,\ 996.00}{280,638.95}$$

$$= K10\ 000\ 000 \times 18.393726617$$

$$= \underline{K183,\ 937,\ 261.70}$$

Note: Same information yields different results due to differences in payment intervals. A whole life annuity due is one payment interval more hence we computed net single payment of K10 000 000 more.

Net single premium for an ordinary temporary life annuity is computed by using the following formula

$$\text{Net single premium} = R\ \frac{Nx + 1 - Nx + n + 1}{Dx}$$

Where Dx = age of a person when annuity taken
$\quad\quad Nx + 1$ = age of a person when first payment is made
$\quad\quad Nx + n + 1$ = age of a person when the last payment is made

Example 16

Find the net single premium of an ordinary annuity of K500 000 per year for a person aged 30 which runs for 25 years.

Solution

Here $Nx + 1 = N31$

$N_x + n + 1 = N_{30} + {}_{25} + {}_1 = N_{56}$

$D_x = D_{30}$

R = K500 000

Using net single premium = $R\ \dfrac{Nx + 1\ -\ Nx + n + 1}{Dx}$

$$= \text{K500 000} \times \frac{N_{31} - N_{56}}{D_{30}}$$

$$= \frac{\text{K500 000} \times 10,\ 153{,}479.81 - 2,\ 560828.18}{440,\ 800.58}$$

$$= \frac{\text{K500 000} \times 7,\ 592{,}651.63}{440{,}800.58}$$

$$= \text{K500 000} \times 17.22468612$$

$$= \text{K8, 612,343.058}$$

$$= \underline{\text{K8, 612,343.06}}$$

The net single premium a temporary life annuity due is given by:

$$\text{Net single premium} = \frac{R\ Nx - Nx + n}{Dx}$$

Where Nx = age of annuity now
    Nx + n age of annuitant when final payment is made
    Dx = age of annuitant now
    R = annuity

Example 17

Find the net single premium of a temporary life annuity due of K500 000 per year for an individual now aged 30 which runs for 25 years.

Solution

Nx = N30
Nx + n = N30 + 25 = N55
Dx = D30
R = K500 000

Net single premium = K500 000 $\dfrac{N30 - N55}{D30}$

$$= K500\ 000 \times \frac{10\ 594\ 280.39 - 2\ 754\ 768.79}{440\ 800.58}$$

$$= K500\ 000 \times \frac{7\ 839\ 511.6}{440\ 800.58}$$

$$= K500\ 000 \times 17.78471258$$

$$= K8\ 892\ 356.267$$

$$= K8\ 892\ 356.27$$

Finally, note that Nx and Dx are taken from the fourth and fifth columns of the table.

AN ADDENDUM

Sometimes life annuities may involve more than a lump sum payment but a series of payments up to a specified time as illustrated by the following example:

Example 18

Suppose someone wants to provide for his child's higher education by purchasing what is called a *deferred temporary life annuity certain* on the child's 10th birthday. He wants to provide for payments of K1 000 000 to be made on the child's 17th, 18th, 19th, 20th and 21st birthday contingent upon his remaining alive. If money is worth 5% compounded annually. How much should he invest on his child's 10th birthday?

Solution

This is an example of a deferred temporary life annuity. As usual we need to find the present values of the payments and the associated probabilities that a child aged 10 will still be alive at 17, 18, 19, 20 and 21 as follows:

- P17 = $\frac{L17}{L10}$ = $\frac{958\ 098}{971\ 804}$ = 0.9858 96333

- P18 = $\frac{L18}{L10}$ = $\frac{955\ 942}{971\ 804}$ = 0.983677778

- P19 = $\frac{L19}{L10}$ = $\frac{953\ 743}{971\ 804}$ = 0.981414976

- P20 = $\frac{L20}{L10}$ = $\frac{951\ 483}{971\ 804}$ = 0.0976710324

- P21 = $\frac{L21}{L10}$ = $\frac{949\ 171}{971\ 804}$ = 0.976710324

Present values are K100 000 $(1.05)^{-7}$, K1000 000 $(1.05)^{-8}$, K1000 000 $(1.05)^{-9}$, K1000 000 $(1.05)^{-10}$ and K1000 000 $(1.05)^{-11}$.

Thus, the amount that should be invested on the child's 10th birthday is given by:

K1000 000 $(1.05)^{-7}$ (0.985896333) + K1000 000 $(1.05)^{-8}$ (0.983677778)

+ K1000 000 $(1.05)^{-9}$ (0.981414976) + K1000 000 $(1.05)^{-10}$ (0.97089404)

+ K1000 000 $(1.05)^{-11}$ (0.976710324).

= K700, 658.1173 + K665, 791.8397 + K632, 628.844 + K601, 075.9615 +

K571, 062.2979

= K3, 171,217.06

So the man must invest K3, 171,217.06 on the child's 10th birthday so that he will get K1000 000 on his 17th, 18th, 19th, 20th and 21st birthday, provided in each case that he is still alive.

LIFE INSURANCE

A life insurance policy is a contract between a life insurance company (the insurer) and an individual (the insured). Insurance companies work on the principal of "Pooling of risks" where the insured has to pay premiums to the insurer from which the insurance company pays the insured after the incident. For life policies, the beneficiaries who may not be the insured are involved as well.

TYPES OF LIFE INSURANCE POLICIES

Life insurance policies may be categorized under the following:

- *Whole life insurance* in which the company promises to pay the face of the policy to the beneficiary upon the death of the insured, whenever that may occur.

- *Term insurance* in which the company promises to pay the face of the policy to the beneficiary upon the death of the insured only if the insured dies within a given number of years after the policy was issued.

- *Endowment insurance* in which the company promises to pay the face of the policy to the beneficiary upon the death of the insured if the, insured dies within a given period after the policy was issued and to pay the face of the policy to the insured at the end of a given number of years if he survives the period.

NET SINGLE PREMIUM FOR WHOLE LIFE INSURANCE

The net single premium for whole life insurance is given by:

$$\text{Net single premium} = I\,\frac{Mx}{Dx}$$

Where Mx = age when policy is purchased
   Dx = age when the amount is received
    I = face value of the policy purchased.

Example 19

At age 26 Joel inherits K50 million. How much whole life insurance can be purchased using the entire sum on net single premium.

Solution

Here Mx = M26
     Dx = D26
       I = face value of the policy purchased

$$I\,\frac{M26}{D26} = K50\ 000\ 000$$

Making I the subject of the formula:

$$I = K50\ 000\ 000 \times \frac{D26}{M26}$$

$$= K50\ 000\ 000 \times \frac{492\ 814.61}{188\ 277.4101}$$

$$= K50\ 000\ 000 \times 2.617491975$$

$$= \underline{K130,\ 874,598.70}$$

NET SINGLE PREMIUM FOR A TERM INSURANCE

The net single premium for a term insurance is given by the following formula:

$$\text{Net single premium} = I \, \frac{Mx - Mx + n}{Dx}$$

Where Mx = age of a person when the policy is purchased
  Mx + n = age of the person when the policy matures i.e. when payment is
    received
    I = face value of the policy
    Dx = age of a person when the policy is issued

Example 20

Find the net single premium for a 20 year term insurance policy of a
K1000 000 issued to a [person aged 25.

Solution

Here Mx = M25
    Mx + n = M25 + 20 = 45
    Dx = D25

Using net single premium = $I \, \dfrac{Mx - Mx + n}{Dx}$

$$= K1000\ 000 \, \frac{(M25 - M45)}{D25}$$

$$= K1000\ 000 \, \frac{(189700.8750 - 154736.6133}{506\ 594.02}$$

$$= K1000\ 000 \times \frac{34\ 964.2617}{506\ 594.02}$$

$$= K1000\ 000 \times 0.069018307$$

$$= K69,\ 018.3072$$

$$= \underline{K69,\ 018.31}$$

NET SINGLE PREMIUM FOR AN ORDINARY TERM LIFE

The net annual premium for an ordinary term life insurance i.e. where
premium is paid at the end of the payment interval is given by the following
formula:

$$\text{Net annual premium} = I \, \frac{Mx - Mx + n}{Nx - Nx + n}$$

Where I = face value of the policy

    Mx = age of a person when policy is purchased

    Mx + n = age of a person when payment received

    Nx = age of a person when policy issued

    Nx + n = age of a person when payment received.

Example 21

Find the net annual premium for an ordinary 20 years term insurance policy of K1000 000 issued to a person aged 25.

Solution

Here Mx = 25

    Mx + n = M20 + 20 = M45

    Nx = N25

    Nx + n = N25 + 20 = N45

Using net annual premium $= \dfrac{Mx - Mx + n}{Nx - Nx + n}$

$$= K1000\ 000 \dfrac{(M25 - M45)}{N25 - N45}$$

$$= K1000\ 000 \dfrac{(189\ 700.8750 - 154736.6133)}{12\ 992\ 619.10 - 5\ 161\ 996.00}$$

$$= K1000\ 000 \dfrac{(34\ 964.2617)}{7,830,623.1}$$

$$= K1000\ 000 \times 0.0004465067627$$

$$= K4,\ 465.067627$$

$$= \underline{K4,\ 465.07}$$

Again notice the difference to the solutions using the same information (example 19 and 20).

NET SINGLE PREMIUM FOR AN ENDOWMENT INSURANCE

The net single premium for an endowment insurance is given by the following formula

$$\boxed{\text{Net single premium} = I\ \dfrac{Mx - Mx + n + Dx + n}{Dx}}$$

Where I = face value

    Mx = age of a person when policy is purchased

    Mx + n = age of a person when payment is received

Dx = age of a person when policy issued
Dx + n = age of a person when policy matures

Example 22

Find the net single premium for a 20 years endowment insurance policy of K1000 000 issued to a person aged 25.

Solution

I = K1000 000
Mx = 25
Mx + n = M25 + M20 = M45
Dx = D25
Dx + n = D25 + 20 = D45

Using Net Single Premium = $I \frac{(Mx - Mx + n + Dx + n)}{Dx}$

$$= K1000\ 000 \left(M25 - M45 + \frac{D45}{D25} \right)$$

$$= K1000\ 000\ \frac{(189700.8750 - 154736.6133 + 280\ 638.95)}{506\ 594.02}$$

$$= K1000\ 000 \times \frac{315\ 603.2117}{506\ 594.02}$$

$$= K1000\ 000 \times 0.622990401$$

$$= K622\ 990.40$$

$$= \underline{K622\ 990.40}$$

NET SINGLE PREMIUM FOR AN ORDINARY ENDOWMENT INSURANCE POLICY

The net single premium for an ordinary endowment insurance policy is given by the following formula:

Net Single Premium = $I \frac{(Mx - Mx + n + Dx + n)}{Nx - Nx + n}$

Where
Mx = age of a person when policy purchased
Mx + n = age of a person when payment is received
Dx + n = age of a person when policy matures
Nx = age of a person when policy issued
Nx + n = age of a person when payment is made.

Example 23

Find the net annual premium for an ordinary 20 years endowment insurance policy of K1000 000 issued to an individual aged 25.

Solution

Here Mx = M25

$\quad$ Mx + n = M25 + 20 = M45

$\quad$ Dx + n = D25 + 20 = D45

$\quad$ Nx = N25

$\quad$ Nx + n = N25 + 20 = M45

$\quad$ I = face value of the policy

Using Net Single Premium = I $\underline{(Mx - Mx + n + Dx + n)}$
$$\quad\quad\quad\quad\quad\quad\quad\quad\quad\quad Nx - Nx + n$$

$\quad\quad$ = K1000 000 $\underline{(M25 - M45 + D45)}$
$$\quad\quad\quad\quad\quad\quad\quad\quad N25 - N45$$

$\quad\quad$ = K1000 000 $\underline{(189700.8750 - 154736.6133 + 280\,638.95)}$
$$\quad\quad\quad\quad\quad\quad\quad\quad 12\,992\,619.10 - 5161\,996.00$$

$\quad\quad$ = K1000 000 X $\underline{315\,603.2117}$
$$\quad\quad\quad\quad\quad\quad\quad 7\,830\,623.10$$

$\quad\quad$ = K1000 000 X 0.040303716

$\quad\quad$ = K40 303.71628

$\quad\quad$ = $\underline{K40\,303.72}$

PROGRESS CLINIC 10

1.$\quad$ As part of a promotional scheme, a bank offers a first prize of K80 000 and a second prize of K30 000 to persons willing to try a new product (distributed without charge) and send in their names on the label. The winners will be drawn at random in front of a ZNBC Television audience.

$\quad\quad$ a) What would be each entrant's expectation if 1,500,000 persons were to send in their names .

$\quad\quad$ b) Would this make it worthwhile to spend K10 000 postage it costs to send in an entry?

2.$\quad$ On his 64th birthday, a person wants to buy an annuity which will provide annual payments of K10 000 000 from his 65th through 70th birthdays, inclusive, provided in each case that he is still alive. If the interest rate is 0.06 compounded semi-annually, what single net premium will he have to pay for this temporary ordinary life annuity?

3.   An importer is offered a shipment of bananas for $6000, and the probabilities that he will be able to sell them for $7000, $6500, $6000,, or $5500 are respectively, 0.25, 0.46, 0.19and 0.10. If he buys the shipment, what is his expected gross profit?

4.   The following table gives the probabilities that a customer who enters the bank hall will lodge in 0,1, 2, 3, or 4 complaints:

Number of complaints	0	1	2	3	4
Probability	0.42	0.36	0.10	0.08	0.04

How many complaints can a customer entering the bank hall be expected to lodge in?

5.   A pure endowment is a policy which pays a person a specified amount after a fixed number of years provided he is still alive.

a) Explain why the net single premium a person of age x has to pay for a pure endowment pay A Kwacha after n years is.

$$A \left(1 + \frac{r}{m} \right)^{-mn} \qquad \left(\frac{Lx + n}{Lx} \right)$$

Where the interest rate is r, compounded m times a year

b)   Find the net single premium for a 15-year pure endowment of K50 000 000 issued to a person aged 45, if money pays 7% compounded annually.

c)   Find the net single premium for a 10-y7ear pure endowment of K12 000 000 issued to a person aged 32, if money pays 8% compounded quarterly.

d)   Find the net single premium for an 18- year pure endowment of K6000 000 issued to a person aged 47. If money pays 6% compounded semi-annually.

6. Using the mortality tables

a) What is the probability that a person aged 36 will still be alive at age 50. What is the probability that a person aged 28 will die within a year.

b) What is the probability that a person aged 20 will still be alive at age 25. What is the probability that a person aged 20 will no longer be alive at age 35.

c) What are the probabilities that a person aged 28 will die before he is 48 and that a person aged 28 will die before he is 35.

d) What are the probabilities that a person aged 25 will be alive at age 50 and that he will be alive at age 60.

e) Find the probabilities that a person aged 15 will be alive at age 45 but die before he is 50 and that a person aged 62 will be alive at age 70 but die before he is 72.

7. Using the mortality tables, find the probability that Mark now aged 30

   a) will attain age 45
   b) will not attain age 65
   c) will attain age 45 but not 65
   d) will die at age 75

8. Find the probability that John age 20:

   a) will live for at least one year
   b) will live for at least 30 years

CHAPTER 11

PREMIER COLLEGE OF BANKING AND FINANCE

BANKING AND FINANCE CERTIFICATE

BF 150 FINANCIAL MATHEMATICS   **(10:30 – 12:30 Hours)**

INSTRUCTIONS TO CANDIDATES

1. Attempt any three (3) out of four (4) questions
2. All questions carry 20 marks
3. Relevant working should be clearly shown.

Question 1

a)   Mr. Kalaki has just received his gratuity as a post columnist amounting to K60 million. He wishes to invest K50 million of the gratuity. He is now faced with a choice between two investment opportunities A and B. Capital outlay for each is K50 million.

A is estimated to yield an annuity of K20 million at the end of each year receivable every five years.

B yields K11 million receivable at the year end in perpetuity.
If the discounting rate is estimated at 20% for Mr. Kalaki;

1) Evaluate the two (2) investment opportunities using net present value (NPV) method.

(10 marks)

2) Recommend with a reason which one of the two (2) investment opportunities Mr. kalaki should choose.

(3 marks)

b)   The terms for a 5 year lease agreement are that K10 million must be paid at the beginning of the first year, to be followed by four equal installments at the beginning of years two, three, four and five at a discount rate of 8%. If the present value of the four equal payments is K26, 496,000, what is the total amount to be paid during the lease? (7 marks)

(Total 20 marks)

Question 2

a) Calculate the effective annual rate of interest of:

    1) 1.5% per month, compound   (2 marks)
    2) 4.5% per quarter, compound   (2 marks)
    3) 9% per half year, compound.   (1 mark)

b) A government bond of K1million is advertised to become K1.54 million after 5 years. Calculate the effective annual rate of interest to one decimal place.

(5 marks)

c) A machine assumes to depreciate at a fixed rate of 12% per annum, will have a book value of K9 288 080 in six years time. What is its purchase value?

(5 marks)

d) If K40 000 000 invested for 5 years yields a simple interest of K3,800,000, what will be the interest on K24,000,000 invested at the same rate for 7.5 years?

(5 marks)

(Total 20 marks)

Question 3

a) Find the sum of the first seven (7) terms of the series;

1) 4, 16, 64 ....   (3 marks)
2) 3, 1, 1/3, ...(3 marks)

b) Find the sum of the first 20 terms of an arithmetic series whose
   first term, a, is –7 and common difference, d, is 3.5.

(3 marks)

c) A food processing company gradually closes down the production of
   tomatoes sauce when winter season comes. If the quantity of
   sauces produced is 12 000 bottles per week and reduction is at a
   rate of 15% each week and 250 kg of potatoes are increasing by
   110 kg each for 8 weeks, calculate

1) The number of bottles of sauce and kg of potatoes produced in week 6
   of the winter season.   (3 marks)

2) The number of weeks taken for production of sauce to drop to 200
   bottles per week.   (3 marks)

3) The total weight of potatoes processed in 9 weeks.   (5 marks)

(Total 20 marks)

Question 4

a) An initial investment of K75 000 000 in a business guarantees the
    following cash flow:

Year	Cash flow
3	K24 000 000
4	K30 000 000
5	K42 000 000

Assume an interest rate of 4.5% compounded semi annually.

1) Find the NPV of the cashflows   (10 marks)
2) Is the investment profitable   (4 marks)

b) Evaluate the following:

1) $125^{-\frac{1}{3}}$

2) $(18.6)^{-2.6}$

3) 5.436 x 0.31 using logs   (6 marks)

(Total 20 marks)

END OF MOCK 1

GOOD LUCK!!!!

PREMIER COLLEGE OF BANKING AND FINANCE

BF150 FINANCIAL MATHEMATICS

WEEKLY CLINICS No.1 November 2006

Instructions: Answer all questions

1. Express:

    a) 0.625 as a fraction
    b) 125/1000 as a percentage
    c) 0.375 as a fraction
    d) 316 as a decimal   (10 marks)

2. A customer `s balance in a savings account increased from K765.20 Cr to K1111.45 Cr over a period. What is the percentage increase to 2 decimal places?

                (4 marks)

3. A firm makes 1376 CD players. The number of Walkman, mini and mid-sized modes is in the ratio 5 to 16 to 11.

    a) How many walkman CD players are made?   (3 marks)
    b) How many of the mid CD players are made?   (3 marks)

4. Change the subject of the formula to the one in brackets for each of the following:

    a) A = 0.5bh (h)
    b) A =   r^2 (r)
    c) P = 2w + 2L (L)   (10 marks)

5. Solve for x

    a) 2x + 7 = x + 9

    b) $\dfrac{2}{3x} = \dfrac{1}{2}$

    c) -11x = -55   (10 marks)

6. Consider the formula

$$K = \frac{J}{R - 2(M + R)}$$

a) If $K = 8$, $R = 1$ and $M = \frac{1}{2}$, what is the value of J?

b) Using the same value of K, what is $\sqrt{k^2 + \frac{k}{2}}$

(10 marks)

7. Work out the following using your calculator as necessary.

a) $(18.6)^{2.6}$

b) $(18.6)^{-2.6}$

c) $\sqrt[2.6]{18.6}$

d) $(14.2)^4 \times (14.2)^{1/4}$

e) $(14.2)^4 + (14.2)^{1/4}$

(10marks)

8. a) Suppose Tom and Dick wish to share K20 000 out in the ratio 3:2. How much will each receive?

(6 marks)

b) A certain amount is to be shared between Tom and Dick for a Pick-a-lot draw in the ratio 70% to 30% respectively. If Dick receives K24, 000, 000, what is the total amount being shared? How much will Tom receive?

(6 marks)

9. a) An item, which cost the retailer K75, 000, is sold at a profit of 25% on the selling price. What is the profit?

b) Solve the simultaneous equation

$$5x + 2y = 34$$
$$x + 3y = 25$$

PREMIER COLLEGE OF BANKING AND FINANCE

CERTIFICATE IN BANKING AND FINANCE

BF 150 – FINANCIAL MATHEMATICS

PROGRESS TEST 2

FRIDAY 9TH MARCH 2007   (1030-1230 HOURS)

INSTRUCTIONS TO CANDIDATES

1. Answer any of **two** out of **three** questions in this paper.
2. All questions carry 20 marks each.
3. Relevant working should be clearly shown.

DO NOT TURN

QUESTION 1

a) Derive the formula for the present value of an annuity (A):

$$A = R \left[\frac{1 - (1 + r)^{-n}}{r} \right]$$

Where A is the present value of an ordinary annuity R per payment period for n periods at an interest rate of r per period.

(6 marks)

b) Mr. Brown has taken out a K30 000 000 mortgage from a local Building Society over 25 years. Interest is to be charged at 12% per annum. Calculate the monthly repayments.

(7 marks)

c) Zam bank grants a loan of K3 000 000 at 7% per annum to Mr. Investor Kantemba. Mr. Kantemba is to repay the loan by paying an annuity of K427 132. 51. How many installments does he need to fully repay the loan.

(7 marks)
(Total 20 marks)

QUESTION 2

Mr. Tembo has just bought a combine harvester which has a life of ten years. At the end of ten years a replacement combine harvester will cost K100 000 000 and he would like to provide for this future commitment by setting up a sinking fund into which equal annual investments will be made, starting now. The fund will earn interest at 10% per annum. Calculate:

a) The annual investment   (10 marks)

b) Construct a schedule and use it to read of the total investment after the 5th payment.   (10 marks)

QUESTION 3

b) A 5-year government bond valued at K5 000 000 is purchased when the market rate of interest is 9%

   i) Calculate the annual repayment (coupon payment) made to the bondholder at the end of each year.

   ii) Calculate the market price of this bond.   (5 marks)

c) John has the following choices of investing his K30 000 000 gratuity:

   i) Placing it in a savings account paying 5% interest compounded semi-annually.

ii) Investing in a business such that the value of the investment after 8 years is
K48 000 000. Which is a better choice?

(5 marks)

d) A machine costing K25, 650, 000 depreciates to a scrap value of K500 000 in 10 years. Calculate:

i) Annual percentage rate of depreciation if the reducing balance method of depreciation is used.

ii) The book value at the end of the 6th year.   (5 marks)

e) Two banks quote the following nominal interest rates: Bank A charges interest on a loan at 9.90% compounded semi-annually and bank B charges 9.75% on a loan compounded quarterly. As a financial analyst, which bank would you recommend a borrower?

(5 marks)
(Total 20 marks)

END OF PROGRESS TEST 2
BON VOYAGE!

PREMIER COLLEGE OF BANKING AND FINANCE

CERTIFICATE IN BANKING AND FINANCE

BF150   Financial Mathematics

MOCK EXAM

Monday 6th April 2007,   **10:30 - 13:30 hours**

Instructions to Candidates

1. Attempt any five (5) out of six (6) Questions
2. All questions carry 20 marks
3. Relevant working should be clearly shown

Question One

a) A house is bought for K50 000 000 down and K50 000 000 a month
  For 14 months. If interest is charged at 12% compounded monthly,
    what is the cash price of a house?

(10 marks)

b) Find the present value of an annuity K300 000 for five years using
   compound interest at 4% per annum, the first receipt being in one
   year's time.

(5 marks)

c) What will be the salary of a bank clerk in 5 year's time, given that she
   earns K8 000 000 now and wage inflation is expected to be 10% per
   annum.

(5 marks)
(Total 20 marks)

Question Two

The following two capital projects, involve the purchase, use and final disposal
of two machines A and B.

	Initial Cost	Net Cash Flows			
		Year 1	Year2	year 3	Year 4
Machine A	50 000	25 500	24 500	17 000	14 000
Machine B	45 000	12 500	15 500	21 000	38 000

Note that year 4 includes scrap values of K5 000 for machine A and
K4 000 for machine B.

Choose between the two projects using each of the following method in firm:

a) Net Present Value – using a cost of capital of 22% and 28%.

(10 marks)

b) Internal Rate of Return – estimate its value using results of (a).

(10 marks)
(Total 20 marks)

Question Three

a) i) Calculate the 6th term and sum of the first 10 numbers of the
   following series: 5, 7.5, 11.25, ...

(4 marks)

ii(A new company makes 250 products in the first week. If the rate
   at which these are produced increases by 6 each week. Find:

- How many will be produced in the 40th week of manufacture.

  (4 marks)

- The expected total produced after 12 weeks.

  (4 marks)

b) Using the mortality tables, find the probability that Mark now aged 30:

i)   will attain age 45
ii)   will not attain age 65
iii) will attain age 45 but not 65
iv)   will die at age 75

(8 marks)

(Total 20 marks)

Question Four

a). A K5 000 000, 4% bond is redeemable at par on July 1, 1990, but may be redeemable on July 1, 1980 or at any other interest payment date thereafter.

i)   Find the purchase price on July 1, 1963 to yield at least 4% compounded semi-annually.

(8 marks)

ii)   Find the investor's profit if the bond is redeemed on July 1, 1985.

(7 marks)

b) A new machine which cost K8 000 000 is depreciated at 8% per annum. What is the book value of the new machine when it is 5 years old?

(5 marks)

(Total 20 mark

Question Five

A machine valued at K12500 000, with a 6 year life is estimated to have a scrap value of K450 000. If the depreciation fund earns 8% p.a.

a) Use the sinking fund method based on ordinary annuity to find the annual deposit into the fund.

(7 marks)

b) Prepare a depreciation schedule.   (8 marks)

c) During what year does the value of the machine reach 50% of its original value?   (5 marks)

(Total 20 marks)

Question Six

a) Suppose a bank grants a loan of K3 000 000 at r% per annum. The borrower is to repay the loan by paying an annuity of K427 132.51 in 10 equal annual instalments. Find the interest rate, r, for the loan.

(10 marks)

b) On his 55th birthday, John uses K25 000 000 of his savings to purchase a pure endowment payable if and when he attains age 85. Assuming he survives, how much will he receive on a 3.5% basis?

(10 marks)

(Total 20 marks)

END OF MOCK
GOOD LUCK

CHAPTER 12

SOLUTIONS TO PROGRESS CLINICS

This chapter provides the suggested solutions to all the progress clinics. Some are abbreviated while others are detailed with complete working. This is purely the author's s desire and design.

SUGGESTED SOLUTIONS TO PROGRESS CLINIC 1

1. a) 1.289×10^{2}

   b) 1.38×10^{-4}

   c) 1.26894×10^{4}

   d) 1.7×10^{-6}

   c) 1.3250499×10^{7}

2. a) 3166.7　　　　b) 0.0172　　　　c) 25772

   d) 0.000029948　　e) 62850 000　　f) 0.00000899931

3. a) 0.052 (T))　　　　b) $8\overline{1}$ (R)

   c) $0.5\overline{3}$ (R)　　　　d) $0.\overline{238095}$ (R)

   e) 0.35 (T)　　　　f) 0.0390625 (T)

   g) $0.29\overline{1}6$ (R)　　　h) 0.1936 (T)

   j) $0.3\overline{52}$ (R)

4. a) ⅝

   b) 12.5%

   d) ⅜

   e) 0.5

   f) 375%

   g) 75%

5. Percentage increase = $\dfrac{\text{New figure – old figure}}{\text{Old figure}} \times 100$

   $= \dfrac{\text{K11 11450 – K765 200}}{\text{K765 200}} \times 100$

= 45.25%

6. Percentage decrease = New figure – old figure X 100
Old figure

= K765 200 – K1111450 X 100
K1111450

= 31.15%

7. K6, 954,750

8. 5 + 16 + 11 = 32

a) walkman CD players: $\frac{5}{32}$ X 1376 = 215

b) Mid-sized CD players: $\frac{11}{32}$ X 1376 = 473

9. a) 3 + 2 = 5

Tom's share = $\frac{3}{5}$ X K20 000 000 = K12, 000,000

Dick's share = $\frac{2}{5}$ X K20 000 000 = K8 000 000

b) 70% + 30% = 100%

Dick's share = $\frac{70}{100}$ X K80 000 000 = K56, 000, 000

10. 8 + 5 + 1 = 14

Yu will receive: $\frac{8}{14}$ X K700 000 = K400,000

11. a) 1998.635766

b) 0.0005003412913

c) 3.078039646

d) 78 926.976

e) 40 660.63081

f) -3

12. Taking y to be weekly wage and x to be number of items sold

y = 100 000 + 5000x
y = 100 000 + 5000 (20) = K200 000

13. a) 4.7

    b) 1.7

    c) -10.5 (Hint: first divide $(17x - 3.8)$ each side)

    d) $\dfrac{3}{4}$

    e) 2

    f) 5

14. a) $h = \dfrac{2A}{b}$

    b) $r = \sqrt{\dfrac{A}{\pi}}$

    c) $L = \dfrac{P - 2w}{2}$ or $\dfrac{P}{2} - w$

15. a) i) J = ⁻16

    ii) 66

    b) $\underline{10}\,S^{\,2}$

    c) Total cost = 6000 + 0.5 (3000) = K7500.00

16. a) $\dfrac{20}{100}$ X K2 5000 000 = K5000, 000.

    b) $\dfrac{10}{100}$ X K2 5000 000 = K2, 500,000

    c) After cash discount of K5000,000, K20 000 000 remains from which we deduct 10% trade discount.

    $\dfrac{10}{100}$ X K20 000 000 = K2000 000

    Thus, Mr. Price has to pay K20 000 000 – K2 000 000 = K18 000 000

17. a) The student will enjoy K50 000 discount per subject for a total of K200 000 for 4 subjects. The student should pay

    [K700 000 X 4} – K2 00 000

    = K2, 600 000

    b) For the second college, the student should pay K400 000 X 4 = K1,600,000

The college in (a) above charges higher tuition fees of K1000 000 more than the college in (b).   Holding other factor constant, I would recommend the student to do his studies at the second college for it is cheaper

SUGGESTED SOLUTIONS TO PROGRESS CLINIC 2

1. (a) $\dfrac{2^3 \times 2^8}{2^5 \times 2^2} = \dfrac{2^{11}}{2^7} = 2^{11-7} = 2^4 = 16$

   (b) $\dfrac{7^6 \, 7^{-10}}{7^3 \, 7^{-8} \, 1} = \dfrac{7^{-14}}{7^{-5}} = 7^{(-4)-(-5)} = 7^1 = 7$

   (c) $(81^3)^4 = (53)\,441)\,{}^{1\!/\!4} = \sqrt[4]{531\,441} = 27$

   Or $\left(\sqrt[4]{81} \right)^3 = 27$

   (d) $\sqrt[3]{125} = 5$

   (e) $\dfrac{1}{\sqrt[3]{125}} = \dfrac{1}{5}$

   (f) $\left(\dfrac{1}{\sqrt[5]{32}} \right)^3 = \dfrac{1}{2^3} = \dfrac{1}{8}$

2. (a) x^4

   (b) $\dfrac{1}{81\,x^2\,y}$

   (c) $\dfrac{-3}{4}$

3. a) $\dfrac{5}{2}$

   b) 125

c) $\dfrac{1}{125}$

c) 32

4. a) ‑5

   b) ‑2

   c) $3x^3$

   d) $\dfrac{-3}{4}$

SUGGESTED SOLUTIONS TO PROGRESS CLINIC 3

1. a) $x = \log_7 9$

   b) $4 = \log_b 15$

   c) $\frac{1}{3} = \log_{12} y$

   d) $\frac{1}{3} = \log_5 112$

   e) $x = \log_3 112$

   f) $7 = \log_b 200$

2. a) $x = \log_2 64 = 64 = 2^x$

   b) $9 = (\frac{1}{3})^x$

   c) $49 = 7^x$

   d) $11 = 11^x$

3. To verify we change the logarithmic functions into exponential functions.

4. a) $n = 7.27$

   b) $n = 10$

5. a) 1.3729

   b) 2.8028

   c) $\overline{3}.3729$

   d) ‑9

   e) 9.9395

f) 0.3201

6. a) 23.6
   (b) 635
   (c) 0.0236
   (d) 0.000000001
   (e) 8 700 000 000 i.e. rounded to the nearest millions
   (f) 209

7. a) 2.17

   b) 2.59

   (c) 8.96

8. (a) 6591

   (b) 3272

   (c) 600

9. 529

10. (a) 19 years

    (b) 14.207

    (c) 11.731

    (d) 7.5%

SUGGESTED SOLUTIONS TO PROGRESS CLINIC 4

1.The question does not specify whether the series is a geometric or an arithmetic one. So to determine which is which we have to test using the principles discussed in the text. Testing for GP: using first and second terms we have:

$5R = 7.5$

$R = \dfrac{7.5}{5} = 1.5$

$A = 5$

$n = 10$

Using $S_n = \dfrac{A(R^n - 1)}{R - 1}$

$$S_{10} = \dfrac{5(1.5^{10} - 1)}{1.5 - 1}$$

$$= \frac{5(56.66503906)}{0.5}$$

$$= 566.6503906$$

$$= \underline{566.65}$$

Using $A R^{n-1}$ for the nth term

$$= 5\,(1.5^{10-1})$$

$$= 5\,(1.5)^9$$

$$= 192.2167969$$

$$= \underline{192.22}$$

b) Using second and third term to test for GP, we have:

$$2.5R = 1.25$$

$$R = \frac{1.25}{2.5}$$

$$= 0.5$$

$$A = 5$$

$$n = 6$$

$$S^6 = \frac{5\,(0.5^6 - 1)}{0.5 - 1}$$

$$= \frac{5(-0.984375)}{-0.5}$$

$$= \frac{-4.921875}{-0.5}$$

$$= \underline{9.84375}$$

6th term $= 5\,(0.5)^{6-1}$

$$= 5\,(0.5)^5$$

$$= 5\,(0.03125)$$

= $\underline{0.15625}$

2. a) Testing for AP using first and second terms

3 + d = 5
d = 2
a = 3
n = 21

Using T_n = a + (n − 1) d
= 3 + (21 − 1) 2
= 3 + (20) (2)
= 43

b) This forms an AP with:

i) a = 250
d = 6
n = 40

40th term = T_{40} = 250 + (40 − 1) 6

= 250 + (39) 6

= 250 + 234

= $\underline{484}$ products

ii) a = 250
d = 6
n = 12

Sum of first 12 using $S_n = \dfrac{n}{2}\left[2a + (n - 1) d \right]$

$= \dfrac{12}{2}\left[2\,(250) + (12 - 1)\,6 \right]$

$= \left[6\,(500) + 66 \right]$

= $\underline{3396}$ products

2. Testing for an AP using first and second

3 + d = 5,   d = 2
a = 3
n = 21

Using $S_n = \dfrac{n}{2}\left[29 + (n - 1)\,d \right]$

$= \dfrac{21}{2}\left[2\,(3) + (21 - 1)\,2 \right]$

3. $S\infty = \dfrac{A}{1-R}$

$8R = {}^-1, \ R = {}^-\frac{1}{8}$
$$A = 8$$

$S\infty = \dfrac{8}{1-\left({}^-\frac{1}{8}\right)}$

$= \dfrac{8}{1+\frac{1}{8}}$

$= \dfrac{8}{\frac{9}{8}}$

$= \dfrac{64}{9} = 7.11\ 11\ 11\ 111$

$= 7.11$

b) $\dfrac{8}{3} R = \dfrac{4}{9}$

$R = \dfrac{4}{9} \times \frac{3}{8} = \dfrac{1}{6}$

$A = \dfrac{8}{3}$

$S\infty = \dfrac{\frac{8}{3}}{1-\frac{1}{6}}$

$= \dfrac{\frac{8}{3}}{\frac{5}{6}}$

$\dfrac{8}{3} \times \dfrac{6}{5} = \dfrac{48}{15} = \underline{3.2}$

c) $5R = {}^-1$

$R = \dfrac{{}^-1}{5}$

$A = 5$

$$S_\infty = \frac{5}{1 - \left(\frac{-1}{5}\right)}$$

$$= \frac{5}{1 + \frac{1}{5}}$$

$$= \frac{5}{\frac{6}{5}}$$

$$= \frac{25}{6} = 4.166666667$$

$$= \underline{4.167}$$

4. Using $S_n = \frac{A\,(R^n - 1)}{R - 1}$

$R = 1.08$
$n = 6$
$S_n = K12\ 500\ 000 - K450\ 000 = K12\ 050\ 000$

$K12\ 050\ 000 = \frac{A\,(1.08^6 - 1)}{1.08 - 1}$

$K12\ 050\ 000\ (0.08) = A\ (0.586874322)$

$A = \frac{K964\ 000}{0.586874322} \qquad = \underline{K1,\ 642,\ 600.407}$

Thus, depreciation charge is approximately K1, 642,600

5. $S_n = \frac{n}{2}\left[2a + (n - 1)d\right]$

$n = 20$
$a = {}^-7$
$d = 3.5$

Thus, $\frac{20}{2}\left[2\,(-7) + (20 - 1)\,3.5\right]$

$11\left[{}^-14 + (19)\,3.5\right]$

$10\left[{}^-14 + 66.5\right]$

$= \underline{525}$

b) i) $R = 4$
   $A = 4$

n = 7

Using $S_n = \dfrac{A\,(R^n - 1)}{R - 1}$

$S_7 = \dfrac{4\,(4^7 - 1)}{4 - 1}$

= $\underline{21844}$

ii) R = ⅓
     A = 3
     n = 7

$S_7 = \dfrac{[3\,(⅓)\,7 - 1]}{⅓ - 1}$

= $\dfrac{^-0.999542752}{^-0.666666666}$ = 1.49931413

= $\underline{1.4993}$

6. a) This is an AP question with

   i) a = K6600 000
      d = K450 000
      n = 3

Using $T_n = a + (n - 1)\,d$

= K6 600 000 + (3 − 1) 450 000

= $\underline{K7,\,500\,000}$

 ii) a = 6 600 000
      d = K450 000
      n = 7

T_7 = K6 600 000 + (7 − 1) 450 000

= K9, 300,000

iii) a = K6 600 000
      d = K450 000
      n = 12

T_{12} = K6 600 000 + (12 − 1) 450 000

= K11, 550,000

b) a = K6 600 000

d = K450 000

n = 10

Using $S_n = \dfrac{n}{2}\left[2a + (n-1)\,d\right]$

$$= \dfrac{10}{2}\left[\,2(6\ 600\ 000) + (10-1)\ 450\ 000\,\right]$$

$$= K86,\ 250,000$$

c) Annual percentage raise of annually indicates the G.P with:

R = 1.04

A = K6 600 000

n = 12

$$S_n = \dfrac{A\,(R^{\,n} - 1)}{R - 1}$$

$$S_{12} = K6\ 600\ 000\ \dfrac{(1.04^{\,12} - 1)}{1.04 - 1}$$

$$= \dfrac{K3,\ 966,812.643}{0.04}$$

$$= \underline{K99,\ 170,\ 316.06}$$

Annual raise of 4% option would be more profitable to Mrs. Clerk as far as her total earnings for the first twelve years are concerned. Annual raise of 4% gives K99, 170, 316.06 – K86, 250, 000 = K12, 920,316.06 more than a guaranteed annual raise of K450 000.

7. a) Since the initial deposit was made on the birthday this is time 0, 1, 2,..............16.

i) a = K100 000

d = K20 000

n = 8 i.e. 7th birthday

Using $T_n = a + (n-1)\,d$

$$T_8 = K100\ 000 + (8-1)\ 20\ 000$$

$$= \underline{K240\ 000} \text{ as the deposit}$$

ii) a = K100 000

d = K20 000

n = 11 i.e. 10th birthday

Hence $T_n = K100\ 000 + (11-1)\ 20\ 000$

$$= \underline{K300\ 000}$$

iii)   a = K100 000
       d = K20 000
       n = 16 i.e 15th birthday

       Hence T_{16} = K100 000 + (16 − 1) 20 000

              = 400 000

a) Here n = 16
        a = K100 000
        d = K20 000

Using S_n = $\frac{n}{2}$ [2a + (n − 1) d]

            = $\frac{16}{2}$ [2 (100 000) + (16 − 1) 20 000]

            = K4, 000,000 as the total deposit

8. 1,925

9. Taking 1994 to be n = 1, then 2003 will be n = 9

    Hence a = K1 527 000 000
            n = 9
            9th term = K2 040 000 000

Using T_n = a + (n − 1) d

        K2 040 000 000 = K1 527 000 000 + (9 − 1) d

        K2 040 000 000 = K1 527 000 000 + 8d

        d = K64, 125 as the required increase each year?

Total for the overall combined non performing loan for the 9 years forms an AP with!

 a = K1 527 000 000
 n = 9
 d = K64 125

Thus, S_n = $\frac{n}{2}$ [2a + (n − 1) d]

S_9 = $\frac{9}{2}$ [2 (1527 000 000) + (9 − 1) 64 125]

    =4.5 [3054 000 000 + 513 000 000]

    = K16, 051,500,000.

10. a) Alternately add 2 and 3: 17, 20 and 22

b) Keep dividing by ⁻2: 2, ⁻1 and ½

b) Keep multiplying by 3: 729, 2, 187 and 6, 561

c) Increase the denominator by 2: $\frac{1}{11}$, $\frac{1}{13}$ and $\frac{1}{15}$

d) Keep adding $\frac{3}{2}$: $\frac{23}{2}$, $\frac{13}{2}$ and $\frac{29}{2}$

e) Keep increasing the number added by 1: 37, 46 and 56.

SUGGESTED SOLUTIONS TO PROGRESS CLINIC 5

1. $(a + b)^9 = a^9 + 9a^8 b + 36a^7 b^2 + 84a^6 b^3 + 126a^5 b^4$

$+ 126a^4 b^5 + 84a^3 b^6 + 36a^2 b^7 + 9ab^8 + b^9.$

2.   (a) 1, 5, 10, 10, 5, 1.

(b) 1, 7, 21, 35, 45, 31, 7, 1.

(c) 1, 9, 36, 84, 126, 126, 84, 36, 9, 1.

3.   (a) $1 + 9x + 27x^2 + 27x^3$

(b) $16x4 + 96x^3y + 216x^2y^2 + 216xy^3 + 81y^4$

(c) $15625x^6 - 37500x^5 + 37500x^4 - 20\,0000x^3 + 6000x^2 - 960x + 64$

4.   (a) $(1.03)^8 = 1^8 + \dfrac{8\,(1)^7\,(0.03)}{1!} + \dfrac{7(8)\,(1)^6\,(0.03)^2}{2!} + \dfrac{6(7)\,(8)\,(1)^5\,(0.03)^3}{3!}$

$= 1 + 0.24 + 0.0252 + 0.001512$

$= 1.266712$

$= 1 + 0.24 + 0.0252 + 0.00152$

$= 1.266712$

(b) $(1.05)^{10} = 1^{10} + \dfrac{10(10\,(1)^9\,(0.05)}{1!} + \dfrac{9\,(10)\,(1)^8\,(0.05)^2}{2!} + \dfrac{8\,(9)\,(10)^7\,(0.05)^3}{3!}$

$= 1 + 0.5 + 0.1125 + 0.015$

$= 1.6275$

5. $(1 - 0.02)^6 = 1^6 + \dfrac{6(1)^5 (-0.02)}{1!} + \dfrac{5(6) (1)^4 (-0.02)}{2!} + \dfrac{4(5) (6) (1)^3 (-0.02)^3}{3!}$

$\qquad + \dfrac{3(4) (5) (6) (1)2 (-0.02)^4}{4!} + \dfrac{2 (3) (4) (5) (6) (1) (-0.02)^5}{5!}$

$\qquad + \dfrac{1 (2) (3) (4) (5) (6) (-0.02)^6}{6!}$

$\qquad = 1 - 0.12 + 0.006 - 0.000016 + 0.0000024$

$\qquad\quad -0.0000000192 + 0.000000000064$

$\qquad = 0.88584238$

$\qquad = 0.886$

6. (a) Using $A = p \left[1 + \dfrac{r}{m} \right]^n$ with p = K5m, r = 0.08, m = 4, n = 40.

$\qquad A = 5000\,000 \left[1 + \dfrac{0.08}{4} \right]^{40} = K11\,040198.32$

(b) $(1 + 0.02)^{40} = \dfrac{1^{40} + 40 (1)^{39} (0.02)}{1!} + \dfrac{39 (40) (1)^{38} (0.02)^2}{2!}$

$\qquad + \dfrac{38 (39) (40) (1)^{37} (0.02)^3}{3!} + \ldots\ldots\ldots\ldots$

$\qquad = 1 + 0.8 + 0312 + 0.07904 + \ldots\ldots\ldots\ldots$

$\qquad = 2.19104$

Thus, K5000 000 x 2.19104) = K10, 955,200.

(c) The difference is K11 040 198.32 – K10 955 200 = K84 998.32

Adding three more terms we have:

$\dfrac{37 (38) (40) (1)^{36} (0.02)^4}{4!} + \dfrac{36(37) (38) (39) (40) (1)^{35} (0.02)^5}{5!}$

$+ \dfrac{35(36) (37) (38) (39) (40) (1)^{34} (0.02)^6}{6!} + \ldots\ldots\ldots$

$= 0.04146224 + 0.0021056256 + 0.00024565632$

$= 0.016973681$

Thus, 0.06973681 + 2.19104 = 2.208013681

K5000 000 x 2.208013681 = K11,040,068.41

The difference now is K11 040 198.32 – K11 040 068.41 = K129.91. Thus, if we add more terms of the expansion the error would have been reduced to less than K1.

7. a) $(1.03)^{-3/2}$ = $1^{-3/2}$ + $\dfrac{(-1/3)\,(1)^{-5/2}\,(0.03)}{1!}$

$+ \dfrac{(-5/3)\,^{(3/2)}\,(1)^{-7/2}\,(0.03)^2}{2!} + \dfrac{(-7/2)\,(-5/2)(-3/2)\,(1)^{-9/2}\,(0.03)^3}{3!} + \ldots$

$= 1 - 045 + 0.0016875 - 0.000059062 + \ldots\ldots$

$= 0.956628438$

$= 0.95663$

b) $(1.03)^{3/2} = 1^{3/2} + \dfrac{(3/2)\,(1)^{\frac{1}{2}}\,(0.03)}{1!} + \dfrac{(\frac{1}{2})\,(3/2)\,(1)^{-\frac{1}{2}}\,(0.03)^2}{2!}$

$+ \dfrac{(-\frac{1}{2})\,(\frac{1}{2})\,^{3/2}\,(1)^{-3/2}\,(0.03)^3}{3!} + \ldots\ldots\ldots$

$= 1 + 0.045 + 0.0003375 - 0.0000016787$

$= 1.045335813$

$= 1.04534$

(c) $(2x + 3y)^{3/2} = (2x)^{3/2} + \dfrac{(3/2)\,(2x)^{\frac{1}{2}}\,(3y)}{1!} + \dfrac{(\frac{1}{2})\,(3/2)\,(2x)^{\frac{1}{2}}\,(3y)^2}{2!}$

$+ \dfrac{(-\frac{1}{2})\,(\frac{1}{2})\,(3/2)\,(2x)^{-3/2}\,(3y)^3}{3!} + \ldots\ldots\ldots$

(d) $(2x + 3y)^{-3/2} = (2x)^{-3/2} + \dfrac{(-3/2)\,(2x)^{-5/2}\,(3y)}{1!} + \dfrac{(-5/2)\,(-3/2)\,(2x)^{-7/2}\,(3y)^2}{2!}$

$+ (-7/2)\,(-5/2)\,(-3/2)\,(2x)^{-9/2}\,(3y)^3 + \ldots\ldots\ldots$

Note: further simplifications for (c) and (d) can still be carried out.

8. (a) $x^2 - 1$ x3   , thus, x remainder $\dfrac{x}{x^2 - 1}$

$\dfrac{^{-}\,x^3 - x}{X}$

(b) Check example 10.

SUGGESTED SOLUTIONS TO PROGRESS CLINIC 6

1. $P(1 + r)^n = 2P$

n = 7.272540909 = 7.27 years

2. $K1000\ 000\ (1 + r)^{15} = K7,500,000$, r = 14.38%

3. Log 2 = 0.301029995

Log 3 = 0.477121254

Log 4 = 0.602059991

Log 1.08 = 0.033423755

Log 1.12 = 0.049218022

Log 1.16 = 0.064457989

Log 1.20 = 0.079181246

Using $P(1 + r)^n = 2P$, $P(1 + r)^n = 3P$ and $P(1 + r)^n = 4P$

Compounded rate	years required for investment to		
	Double	Treble	Quadruple
8%	9.00648453 = 9.01	14.27491477 = 14.27	18.01293694 = 18.01
12%	6.11625444 = 6.12	969403553 = 9.69	12.23251091 =12.23
16%	4. 670173545 = 4.67	7.402049946 = 7.40	9.340345849 = 9.34
20%	3.801784011 = 3.80	6.025685097 = 6.03	7.603568034 =7.60

4. K125 000 000 X 0.07 = K8 750 000

Market price = $K125\ 000\ 000\ (1.1)^{-4} + K8750\ 000 \left[\dfrac{1 - (1.1)}{0.1} \right]^{-4}$

= K113, 113,004.60

5. $S = K9500\ 000\ (1.12)^{12} + \dfrac{800\ 000\ (1.12)^{12} - 800\ 000)}{0.12}$

= K17, 705,265.3

6. a) $F = (P(1 + r)^n$

= $K12\ 500\ 000\ (1.11)^6$ = K23, 380.181.90

b) i) K3108,000
    ii) K2, 850,000

7. Using $S = P(1 + rn)$

K9700 000 = P (1 + 0.085 X 2.5)

P = K8, 000,000

8. Straight-line depreciation

Depreciation charge = $\underline{Cost - Scrap}$
Useful life in years

$= \underline{K160\ 000\ 000}$ = K20 000 000 Pa
8

a)1999 to 2002 is 3 years hence K20 000 000 X 3 = K60 000 00. Thus, K160 000 000 – K60 000 000 = k100 000 000.

b)1999 to 2005 is 6 years hence K20 000 000 X 6 = K120 000 000. Thus, K160 000 000 – K120 000 000 = K40 000 000

9. Using P = A (1 – dn)

= K1500 000 (1 – 0.08 X 2)

= K1, 260,000

10.Using P A (1 – dn)

a) P = K5000 000 $\left[1 - 0.09\ X\ \dfrac{60}{360} \right]$

= K4, 925,000

b) P = K5000 000 $\left[1 - 0.09\ X\ \dfrac{120}{360} \right]$

= K4, 850,000

11.Using S = P (1 + rn)

= K4000 000 (1 + 0.09 X 3)

= K5, 080,000 per year

Hence monthly payments should be $\underline{K5,\ 080,000}$ = $\underline{K141,\ 111.11}$
36

Using $\left(1 + \dfrac{r}{m} \right)^m - 1$

a) 5.0945%   b) 8.16%   c) 9.3807%

K1200 000 $1 + \left[\dfrac{0.08}{4} \right]^8$ – K1000 000

= K405, 991.26 still owed

12.a) Using $= P(1 + r)^n$

$= K6000\,000 (1 + 0.06)^4$

$= K7\,574\,861.76$

b) Using $A = P\left(1 + \dfrac{r}{m}\right)^m$

$K6000\,000 \left(1 + \dfrac{0.06}{2}\right)^8$

$= K7,600,620.49$

c) $K6000\,000 \left(1 + \dfrac{0.06}{4}\right)^{16}$

d) $K6000\,000 \left(1 + \dfrac{0.06}{12}\right)^{48}$

$= K7,622,934.97$

From above it is clear that as the frequency of compounding increases, the value of the investment increases as well for the same number of years at the same interest rate.

13. Using $\quad P = \dfrac{A}{\left(1 + \dfrac{r}{m}\right)^m}$

$= \dfrac{K2000\,000\,000}{\left(1 + \dfrac{0.08}{4}\right)^8}$

$= K1,706,980,742$

14. $P = K1000\,000 + K1000\,000 (1 + 0.00075)^{-12} + K1000\,000$

$(1 + 0.0075)^{-24}$

$= K2,750069.56$

15. a). Using $A = P\left(1 + \dfrac{r}{m}\right)^m$

$= K300\,000\,000 = P\left(1 + \dfrac{0.10}{2}\right)^4$

$= K300\,000\,000 = P(1.05)^4$

$P = K246,810,742.40$

b) Using $ER = \left(1 + \dfrac{r}{m}\right)^m - 1$

$$= \left(1 + \frac{0.10}{2}\right)^2 - 1$$

$$= (1.05)^2 - 1$$

$$= 10.25\%$$

16. a) Using $D = B(1 - r)^n$

$$K12\,000\,000 = K22\,000\,000\,(1 - r)^5$$

$$(1 - r)5 = 0.545454545$$

$$1 - r = 0.88583271$$

$$r = 11.4167289$$

$$= 11.42\%$$

b) $K22\,000\,000\,(1 - 0.114167289)^3$

$$= K15,\,292,\,476.43$$

f) Straight-line method = $\dfrac{\text{Cost} - \text{Scrap}}{\text{Useful life}}$

$$\frac{K22\,000\,000 - K12\,000\,\,000}{5}$$

$= \underline{K2,\,000,\,0000}$ P.a.

Thus, after 3 years the book value would be:

$K22\,000\,000 - 3\,(K2000\,000)$

$= \underline{K16,\,000,000}$

Hence using straight-line method. The book value is
K16 000 000 – K15 292 476. 43 = K707, 523.57 more than using the reducing balance method.

17. Maturity value of debt = $K2500\,000\,(1.12)^4 = K3,\,933,\,798.40$

Present value = $\dfrac{K3,\,933,798.40}{(1.095)^4}$

$$= \underline{K2,\,736,249.04}$$

Thus, real cost of debt = K2, 736,249.04 – K2, 500,000

$$= \underline{K236,\,249.04}$$

SUGGESTED SOLUTIONS TO PROGRESS CLINIC 7

1. a) NPV is computed from cash flows and not profits. Hence the first
        step is to convert the profits into cash flows by **adding** back
        depreciation charge per annum.

$$\text{Depreciation charge} = \frac{\text{Cost} - \text{Scrap Value}}{\text{Useful life in years}}$$

$$= \frac{\text{K400 000 000} - \text{K80 000 000}}{4}$$

$$= \underline{\text{K80 000 000}} \text{ p.a. for both projects.}$$

		Project x		Project y	
Year	Profits K'000	Depreciation K'000	Cash Flows K'000	Profits K'000	Cash Flows K'000
1	160 000	80 000	240 000	60 000	140 000
2	160 000	80 000	240 000	100 000	180 000
3	80 000	80 000	160 000	180 000	260 000
3	40 000	80 000	120 000	240 000	320 000

The NPV computations are as follows:

		Project x		Project y	
Year	DF at 16%	Cash flows K'000	PV K'000	Cash flows K'000	PV K'000
0	1.000	(400 000)	(400 000)	(400 000)	(400 000
1	0.862	240 000	206 808	140 000	120 680
2	0.743	240 000	178 320	180 000	133 740
3	0.641	160 000	102 560	260 000	166 660
4	0.552	120 000	66 240	320 000	176 640
4	0.552	80 000	441 160	80 000	44 160
		NPV	198 160		241 880

Thus, using 3 decimal places for the discount factor, the NPV for project x is
K198 160 while that of project y is K241 880.

b) Project y should be undertaken because it gives a higher positive NPV
    compared to project x.

c) This is the cost to the company of raising finance for capital expenditure
    projects: the cost of shareholders capital and the cost of any loans raised.

2. a) Here cash flows are given hence we ignore depreciation charges.

Year	DF at 12%	Project x Cash lows K'000	PV K'000	Project y Cash flow K'000	PV K'000
0	1.000	(650 000)	(650 000)	(750 000)	(750 000)
1	0.893	150 000	133 950	50 000	44 650
2	0.797	225 000	179 325	100 000	79 700
3	0.712	275 000	195 800	150 000	106 800
4	0.636	75 000	47 700	450 000	286 200
5	0.567	50 000	28 350	300 000	170 100
5	0.567	100 000	57 600	200 000	113 400
		NPV	(7275)		50850

b) ABC should invest in project y as it gives a positive NPV.

c) In investment appraisal only relevant costs are taken into account. Expenditure of K125 million is not a relevant cost but a sunk cost which will have been incurred whether or not a project is undertaken. It is therefore ignored here.

NOTE: In the computations above, the scrap value is taken as an example of a cash in flow and discounted at the end of useful life. Take note.

3. Machine A

Year	Net cash flow	DF at 22%	PV	DF at 28%	PV
0	(50 000)	1.0000	(50 000)	1.000	(50 000)
1	25 500	0.8197	20 902.35	0.7813	199 23.15
2	24 500	0.6719	16 461.54	0.6104	14 954.79
3	17 000	0.5507	9 361.90	0.4768	8 105.00
4	14 000	0.4514	6 319.60	0.3725	5 215.00
		NPV	3045.40		(1 801.45)

Machine B

a) Year	Net cash flow	DF at 22%	PV	DF at 28%	PV
0	(45 000)	1.0000	(45000)	1.0000	(45 000)
1	12 500	0.8197	10246.25	0.7813	9766.25
2	15 500	0.6719	10414.45	0.6104	9461.19
3	21 000	0.5507	11564.70	0.4768	10012.80
4	38 000	0.4514	17153.19	0.3725	14155.00
		NPV	4378.60		1604.75

At a rate of 22% machine B has a higher NPV and thus should be chosen as the best option. Further, at a rate of 28% machine B has a higher positive NPV.

b) Using IRR = A% + $\frac{a}{(a + b)}$ (B – A)%   machine A,

$$IRR = 22\% \left(\frac{+ 3045.40}{3045.40 - (-1801.45)} \right) 28 - 22$$

$$22\% + \left(\frac{3045.40}{4846.85}\right) \quad X\ 6$$

= 25.76 995368

= 25.77%

Machine B: IRR = $22\% + \left(\dfrac{4378.60}{4378.60 - (-1604.75)}\ (28-22)\ \%\right)$

$$= 22\% + \left(\frac{4378.60}{5983.35}\right)\ X\ 6$$

= 26.39078443

= <u>26.39%</u>

Thus, machine B has the higher IRR and should be selected.

4. a) NPV computation

Year	Cash flow K'000	DF at 15%	PV K'000
2007	(21 000)	1.000	(21 000)
2008	(30 000)	0.870	(26 100)
2009	7 500	0.756	5 670
2010	9 000	0.658	5 922
2011	10 500	0.572	6 006
2012 -17	12 000	2.164	25 968

NPV <u>(3534)</u>

Project should not be accepted as it gives negative NPV

b) To compute IRR, we select a lower discount rate which will give us positive NPV, say 10%.

Year	Cash flow K'000	DF at 10%	PV K'000
2007	(21 000)	1.000	(21 000)
2008	(30 000)	0.909	(27 270)
2009	7 500	0.826	6 195
2010	9 000	0.751	6 759
2011	10 500	0.683	7 172
2012 – 17	12 000	2. 975	35 700

NPV <u>7556</u>

Using IRR = A% + $\left[\dfrac{a}{a-b} (B-A)\% \right]$

$$10\% + \left[\dfrac{7556}{7556 - (\text{-}3534)} \ (15-10)\ \% \right]$$

= 13.4%

5. NPV computations

Year	Cash flow K'000	DF at 11%	PV K'000
0	(28 000)	1.0000	(28 000)
1	8 000	0.9009	7207.20
2	8 000	0.8116	6492.80
3	8 000	0.7312	5849.60
		NPV	(8450.40)

Project is not viable as it has negative NPV. Alternatively, we can use annuity formula as follows:

NPV = A $\left[\dfrac{1 - (1+r)^{-n}}{r} \right]$ - cost

$= 8000 \left[\dfrac{1 - (1.11)^{-3}}{0.11} \right]$ - 28 000

= (9913.80)

The difference in the above two solutions is due to rounding off of numbers.

6. IRR = A% + $\dfrac{a\ (B-A)\%}{a-b}$

$= 16\% + \left[\dfrac{14\ 130\ 000}{14\ 130\ 000 - (\text{-}5\ 840\ 000)} \ (20-16)\% \right]$

$= 16\% + \left[\dfrac{14\ 130\ 000}{19\ 970\ 000} \right] \times 4$

= 18.83024537

= 18.83%

NPV computations

7.

Year	PV	DF at 12%	Cash flow	PV	Cash flow	PV	Cash flow	PV	Cash flow	PV
			K'000	K'000	K'000	K'000	K'000	K'000		
0	1.000		(70 000)	(70 000)	(70 000)	(70 000)	(70 000)	(70 000)		
1	0.893		25 000	22 325	16 000	14 288	15 000	13 395		
2	0.797		23 000	18 331	18 000	14 346	17 000	15 781		
3	0.712		18 000	12 816	18 000	12 816	17 000	12 104		
4	0.636		14 000	8 904	16 000	10 176	16 000	10 176		
5	0.567		10 000	5 670	16 000	9 072	15 000	9 072		
6	0.452		8 000	3 616	12 000	5 424	10 000	4 520		
			NPV	1 662		(3 878)		(5 552)		

Project A would be preferable using NPV technique at 12% discount rate since it gives positive NPV.

8. To compute IRR, we need two discount factors which will give us one positive and one negative NPV. Using a rate of 8%.

Year	Cash flow	DF at 8%	PV
0	(13 500 000)	1.0000	(13 500 000)
1	5 000 000	0.9259	4 629 500
2	8 000 000	0.8573	6 858 400
3	3 000 000	0.7938	2 381 400

Since NPV is positive at 8%, we need a higher discount rate to give us a negative NPV. Let's use 11%

Year	Cash flow	DF at 11%	PV
0	(13 500 000)	1.0000	(13 500 000)
2	5 000 000	0.9009	4 504 500
3	8 000 000	0.8116	6 492 800
4	3 000 000	0.7312	2 193 600
	NPV		(309 100)

Using IRR = A% + $\left[\dfrac{a}{a + b} (B - A)\% \right]$

$= 8\% + \left[\dfrac{369\ 300}{369\ 300 - (\text{-}309\ 100)} (11 - 8)\% \right]$

$= 8\% + \dfrac{369\ 300}{678\ 400}\ \text{X}\ 3\%$

= 9.633207309

= 9.63%

NOTE: You can use any discount rates as long as they give you one positive and one negative NPV, above answer will hold.

9. a) NPV at 15%

Year	Cash flow	DF at 15%	PV
0	(50 000 000)	1.000	(50 000 000)
1	18 000 000	0.870	15 660 000
2	25 000 000	0.756	18 900 000
3	20 000 000	0.658	13 160 000
4	10 000 000	0.572	5 720 000
		NPV	(1 256 000)

c) $IRR = A\% + \left[\dfrac{a}{a+b} (B-A)\% \right]$

$= 15\% + \left[\dfrac{3\,440\,000}{3\,440\,000 - (-1256\,000)} (20-15)\% \right]$

$= 15\% + \left[\dfrac{3\,440\,000}{4\,696\,000} \right] \times 5\%$

$= 18.66269165$

$= \underline{18.66\%}$

d) The project is expected to earn a DCF return in excess of the target rate of 17%, so (ignoring risk) on financial grounds it is a worthwhile investment.

SUGGESTED SOLUTIONS TO PROGRESS CLINIC 8

1. This question combines the knowledge you acquired on investment appraisals and annuities.

a) NPV = Present value of inflows – present value of outflows. For investment opportunity A we will need to find the present value of an annuity of K20 million while for investment opportunity B we will find the present value of K11 million in perpetuity.

Present value of K20 million (ordinary annuity)

$PV = A \left[\dfrac{1-(1+r)^{-n}}{r} \right]$ Where A = K20 million
r = 0.20
n = 5

$= K20\,000\,000 \left[\dfrac{1-(1+0.20)^{-5}}{0.20} \right]$

$= K20\,000\,000 \left[\dfrac{1-(1.2)^{-5}}{0.2} \right]$

$= K20\,000\,000\,(2.99061214)$

= K59, 812,242.80

NPV   = K59, 812,242.80 – K50 000 000

= <u>K9, 812,242.80</u>

Present value of K11 million in perpetuity

$$PV = \frac{A}{r}$$ where A = K11 000 000

r = 0.2

Hence PV = $\frac{K11\ 000\ 000}{0.2}$ = K55, 000,000

NPV = K55 000 000 – 50 000 000

= <u>K5 000 000</u>

b) Mr. Kalaki should choose investment opportunity B which gives a profit of K4, 812,242.80 more than investment opportunity A. Note both investment opportunities are viable as they give positive NPV.

2. The question requires us to use the compound interest tabular format, though we can get the same answer using the annuity formula.

a)

Time	Cash flow K'000	Discount factor at 4%	Present value K'000
1	300 000	0.962	288 600
2	300 000	0.925	277 500
3	300 000	0.889	266 700
4	300 000	0.855	256 500
5	300 000	0.822	246 600

Total PV = K1,335,900

Alternatively, using the annuity factor correct to 3 decimal places we have:

$$\text{Annuity factor} = \left[\frac{1 - (1 + r)^{-n}}{r} \right]$$

$$= \left[\frac{1 - (1.04)^{-5}}{0.04} \right]$$

$$= 4.451822325$$

$$= 4.452$$

Hence PV = K300 000 000 X 4.453

$$= \underline{K1, 335,600,000}$$

The difference of about K300 000 is due to rounding off of numbers.

3. This is an example of an annuity due whose present value is found by using:

$$R + \frac{R[1-(1+r)]^{-n}}{r}$$

Letting A be the constant payment made at the beginning of each years two to five, we have:

$$PV = A\left[\frac{1-(1+r)^{-n}}{r}\right] \qquad \text{Where } n = 4$$
$$r = 0.08$$
$$PV = K26\ 496\ 000$$

$$= K26\ 496\ 000 = A\left[\frac{1-(1.08)}{0.08}\right]^{-4}$$

$$= K26\ 496\ 000 = A\ (3.312126838)$$

$$A = \frac{K26\ 496\ 000}{3.312126838}$$

$$= K7, 999,693.64$$

The total is thus K10 000 000 + (7 999 693.64 X 4)

$$= K10\ 000\ 000 + K31, 998,774.56$$

$$= \underline{K41, 998,774.56}$$

4. a) 5.6502

b) 4.8696

c) Here $r = 0.025$ and $n = 6$ (interest periods)

5.5081

d) $r = 0.0125$ and $n = 3$

2.9265

5. a) Present value of a loan of K100 000 000 is K100 000 000 since it is granted now so cannot be discounted.

b) Present value of K100 000 000 in 12 years at 10% is:

PV = K100 000 000 (1.1) $^{-12}$

= <u>K31, 863,081.70</u>

6. Present value of perpetuity is given by:

PV = $\frac{A}{r}$, Thus, $\frac{K4000\ 000}{0.05}$ = <u>K80, 000,000</u>

SUGGESTED SOLUTIONS TO PROGRESS CLINIC 9

The annuity is the coupon payment.

Coupon payment = Coupon rate X face value

= 12% X K30 000 000

= <u>K3, 600 000</u>

2. For semi-annual coupon bond r = $\frac{12\%}{2}$ = 6%

Using coupon payment = Coupon rate X face value

= 6% X K30 000 000

= <u>K1, 800,000</u>

3. Purchase price for a pure bond is given by:

P = F (1 + r) $^{-n}$

= K30 000 000 (1.15) $^{-8}$

= <u>K9, 807,053.22</u>

4. a) This is an annual coupon bond

Face value = $\frac{Coupon\ payment}{Coupon\ rate}$

= $\frac{K10\ 000\ 000}{0.05}$

= <u>K200 000 000</u>

b) r = 0.05, n = 10, I = K10 000 000, M = K200 000 000

Using P = I $\left[\dfrac{1 - (1 + r)^{-n}}{r} \right]$ + M (1 + r) $^{-n}$

$$= K10\,0000\,0000 \left[\frac{1 - (0.05)^{-10}}{0.05} \right] + K200\,000\,000\,(1.05)^{-10}$$

$$= K10\,000\,0000\,(7.721734929) + K200\,000\,0000\,(0.613913253)$$

$$= K77,217,349.29 + K122,782,650.70$$

$$= \underline{K200\,000\,000}$$

5. Here $r = \frac{5\%}{2} = 2.5\%$, n = 10 X 2 = 20

   I = K5 000 000 , M = K200 000 000

   Using $P = I\left[\frac{1 - (1 + r)^{-n}}{r} \right] + M(1 + r)^{-n}$

   $$= K5\,000\,000 \left[\frac{1 - (1.025)^{-20}}{0.025} \right] + K200\,000\,000\,(1.025)^{-20}$$

   $$= K5\,000\,000\,(15.58916229) + K200\,000\,000\,(0.610270942)$$

   $$= K77,945,811.45 + K122,054,188.60$$

   $$= \underline{K200\,000\,000}$$

6. $r = \frac{15\%}{2} = 7.5\%$

   n = 2020 – 19193 = 27 X 2 = 54

   M = K65 000 000

   I = K3, 250,000 i.e. 5% of K65 000 000

   Using

   $$P = I\ \frac{1 - (1 + r)^{-n}}{r} + M(1 + r)^{-n}$$

   $$= K3\,250\,000\ \frac{1 - (1.075)^{-54}}{0.075} + K65\,000\,000\,(1.075)^{-54}$$

   $$= K3\,250\,000\,(13.06487205) + K65\,000\,000\,(0.020134596)$$

   $$= K42,460,834.16 + K1,308,748.772$$

   $$= K43,769,582.93$$

b) By 2015, the book value of the bond will have increased to the purchase price to yield 15% compounded semi-annually on that date.

Here r = $\frac{15\%}{2}$ = 7.5%

n = 2020 – 2015 = 5 years X 2 = 10
M = K65 000 000
I = K3 250 000

Using P = I $\left[\dfrac{1-(1+r)^{-n}}{r}\right]$ + M $\left(1+r\right)^{-n}$

$= K3\,250\,000 \left[\dfrac{1-(1.075)^{-10}}{0.075}\right] + K65\,000\,000\,(1.075)^{-10}$

= K3 250 000 (6.864080956) + K65 000 000 (0.485193928)

= K22,308, 263.11 + K31, 537, 605.34

= K53, 845,868.45

Thus, profit = K65 000 000 – K53 845 868.45

= K11, 154, 131.53

7. M = K30 000 000

$r_1 = \dfrac{12\%}{2}$ = 6% = 0.06

$r_2 = \dfrac{9\%}{2}$ = 45% = 0.045

n = 2½ X 2 = 5

I = 6% X K30 000 000

= K1, 800, 000

We first calculate the purchase price using the following formula:

P = I $\left[\dfrac{1-(1+r)^{-n}}{r}\right]$ + $(1+r)^{-n}$

$= K1\,8000\,000 \left[\dfrac{1-(1.045)^{-5}}{0.045}\right] + K30\,000\,000\,(1.045)^{-5}$

= K1 8000 000 (4.38996744) + K30 000 000 (0.802451046)

= K7, 901, 958.139 + K24, 073,531.40

= K31, 975,489.54 as the purchase price or book value on the purchase date.

The schedule is as follows:

Period	Book value beginning of period	Interest due on book value	Bond Interest payment	Change in book value
1	31 975 489. 54	1 438 897.029	1 800 000	361 102.9707
2	31 614 386. 57	1 422 647.396	1 800 000	377 352.6044
3	31 237 034.15	1 405 666.537	1 800 000	394 333.4635
4	30 842 700.69	1 387 921.531	1 800 000	412 078.4691
5	30 430 622.22	1 369 378	1 800 000	430 622.0001
6	30 000 000.22	-	-	-

This is an example of an amortization bond schedule where we have a premium and the whole process is to reduce the present value of K31 975 489.54 to the face value of K30 000 000.

8. M = K30 000 000

$$r_1 = \frac{9\%}{2} = \$5\% = 0.05$$

$$r_2 = \frac{12\%}{2} = 0.06$$

n = 2 ½ X 2 = 5

I = 4.5% X K30 000 000 = K1 350 000

Using $P = I\left[\dfrac{1 - (1 + r)^{-n}}{r}\right] - M(1 + r)^{-n}$

$$= K1\,350\,000 \left[\frac{1 - (1.06)^{-5}}{0.06}\right] + K30\,000\,000\,(1.06)^{-5}$$

$$= K1\,350\,000\,(4.212363786) + K30\,000\,000\,(0.747258172)$$

$$= K5{,}686{,}691.111 + K22{,}417{,}745.19$$

$$= \underline{K28\,104\,436.30}$$

The schedule is as follows

Period	Book value beginning of Payment	Interest due on book value	Bond interest payment	Change in book value
1	28 104 436.30	1 686 266.178	1 350 000	336 266.178
2	28 440 702.48	1 706 442.149	1 350 000	356 442.1488
3	28 797 144.63	1 727 828.678	1 350 000	377 828.6777
4	29 174 973.31	1 750 498.398	1 350 000	400 498.3985
5	29 575 471.71	1 774 528.303	1 350 000	424 528.3025
6.	30 000 000.01	-	-	-

9. For K25 000 000 bond redeemable in years:

M = K25 000 000

$r = \dfrac{3\%}{2} = 1.5\% = 0.05$

n = 5 X 2 = 10

I = 2.5% of K25 000 000 = K625 000

Using $P = I\left[\dfrac{1-(1+r)^{-n}}{r}\right] + M(1+r)^{-n}$

$= K625\,000\left[\dfrac{1-(1.05)^{-10}}{0.015}\right] + K25\,000\,000\,(1.015)^{-10}$

= K625 000 (9.222184552) + K25 000 000 (0.861667231)

= K5, 763, 865.345 + K21 541 680.79

= K27, 305, 546.14

For K25 000 000 bond redeemable in 6 years

I = K625 000
r = 0.015
n = 12
M = K25 000 000

Thus, $P = K625\,000\left[\dfrac{1-(1.015)^{-12}}{0.015}\right] + K25\,000\,000\,(1.015)^{-12}$

= K625 000 (10.90750521) + K25 000 000 (0.836387421)

= K6, 817, 190.754 + K20 909 685.55

= K27, 726, 876.30

For K50 000 000 bond redeemable in 9 years

I = 2.5% of K50 000 000 = K1 250 000
r = 0.015
n = 18
M = K50 000 000

Using P = K1 250 $\left[\dfrac{1 - (1.015)^{-18}}{0.015} \right]$ + K50 000 000 (1.015)$^{-18}$

= K1 250 000 (15.6725089) + K50 000 000 (0.764911586)

= K19, 590, 636.13 + K38, 245, 579.30

= K57, 836, 215.43

Thus, the purchase price of the serial bond is the present value the three separate bonds.

Hence K27 305 546.14 + K27 726 876.30 + K57 836 215.43

= K112, 868,637.90

SUGGESTED SOLUTIONS TO PROGRESS CLINIC 10

1. a) one name wins K80 000 and the second name wins K30 000 for a total of 110 000. So 1 499 998 names do not attract any prize.

    Average is $\dfrac{K110\ 000}{1\ 500\ 000}$ = K0.073 33333

    This gives the expectation of K7300

    b) No, the expectation is less than the cost of postage.

2. K42,771,340

3. $430 i.e. $\left[(7000 \times 0.25\ +\ (6000 \times 0.19)\ +\ (5500 \times 0.16) \right]$

4. 0.96 complaints i.e. $\left[0.X\ 0.42)\ +\ (1 \times 0.36)\ +\ (2 \times 0.10) \right]$

    + (3 X 0.08) + (4 X 0.04)

5. a) single premium a person has to pay must be connected to the probability of that person still being alive at a given age. Hence the formula given above.

    b) Using A (1 + r)$^{-n}$ $\underline{Lx + n}$

Lx

K50 000 000 $(1 + 0.07)^{-15}$ X $\underline{L60}$
                                      L45

K50 000 000 $(1.07)^{-15}$ X $\dfrac{677\ 771}{852\ 554}$

K18122 300.98 X 0.794988934

$\underline{K14, 407, 028.83}$

c) Using A $\left[1 + \dfrac{r}{m} \right]^{-mn} \cdot \left[\dfrac{Lx + n}{Lx} \right]$

K12 000 000$\left[1 + \dfrac{0.08}{4} \right]^{-40} \cdot \left[\dfrac{L42}{L32} \right]$

K12 000 000$(1.02)^{-40} \cdot \dfrac{872\ 098}{917\ 880}$

= K5, 434, 684. 982 X 0.05012202

= $\underline{K5\ 163, 613.88}$

d) Using A $\left[1 + \dfrac{r}{m} \right]^{-mn} \cdot \left[\dfrac{Lx + n}{Lx} \right]$

K6000 000 $\left[1 + \dfrac{0.06}{2} \right]^{-36} \cdot \left[\dfrac{L65}{L47} \right]$

K6000 000 $(1.03)^{-36}$ X $\dfrac{577\ 882}{837\ 413}$

K2,070, 194.55 X 0.690080044

$\underline{K1,428,599.95}$

6. a). L 50 = 810 900
         L36 = 902 393

         $\dfrac{L50 = 810\ 900}{L36 = 902\ 393}$ = 0.89 861

     b) L28 = 930 788
         L29 = 927 763

         $\dfrac{L28 - L29}{L28}$ = $\dfrac{930\ 788 - 927\ 763}{930\ 788}$ = $\dfrac{3025}{930\ 788}$ = 0.00325

     c) L20 = 915 483
         L25 = 939 197

$$L35 = 906\ 554$$

$$\frac{L25}{L20} = \frac{939\ 197}{951\ 483} = 0.98709$$

d) $L28 = 930\ 788$
$L48 = 829\ 114$
$L35 = 906\ 554$

$$\frac{L28 - L48}{L28} = \frac{930\ 788 - 829\ 114}{930\ 788} = \frac{101\ 678}{930\ 788} = 0.10923$$

$$\frac{L28 - L35}{L28} = \frac{930\ 788 - 906\ 554}{930\ 788} = \frac{24234}{930\ 788} = 0.02604$$

e) $L50 = 810\ 900$
$L25 = 939\ 197$
$L60 = 677\ 771$

$$\frac{L50}{L25} = \frac{810\ 900}{939\ 197} = 0.863397$$

$$\frac{L60}{L25} = \frac{677\ 771}{939\ 197} = 0.72165$$

$$\frac{L50 - L60}{L25} = \frac{810\ 900 - 677\ 771}{939\ 197} = \frac{133\ 129}{939\ 197} = 0.14175$$

f) $L45 = 852\ 554$
$L50 = 810\ 900$
$L15 = 962\ 270$
$L70 = 454\ 548$
$L72 = 400\ 112$
$L62 = 640\ 761$

$$\frac{L28 - L48}{L15} = \frac{852\ 554 - 810\ 900}{962\ 270} = \frac{41654}{962\ 270} = 0.04329$$

$$\frac{L70 - L72}{L62} = \frac{454\ 548 - 400\ 112}{640\ 761} = \frac{54436}{640\ 761} = 0.08496$$

7. $L30 = 924\ 609$

a) $L45 = 852\ 554$

$$^{15}P_{30} = \frac{L45}{L30} = \frac{852\ 554}{924\ 609} = 0.92207$$

b) $^{35}q_{30} = \frac{L30 - L65}{L30} = \frac{924\ 609 - 577\ 882}{924\ 609} = \frac{346\ 727}{924\ 609} = 0.374999$

c) $\frac{L45 - L65}{L30} = \frac{852\ 554 - 577\ 882}{924\ 609} = \frac{274\ 670}{924\ 609} = 0.29707$

d) $d75 = 28\ 009$

$$\frac{d75}{L30} = \frac{28009}{924\ 609} = 0.03029$$

8. a). L20 = 951 483
    L21 = 949 171

$$P_{20} = \frac{L21}{L20} = \frac{949\ 171}{951\ 483} = 0.99757$$

b) L20 = 951 483
    L50 = 810 900

$$_{30}P_{20} = \frac{L50}{L20} = \frac{810\ 900}{951\ 483} = 0.85225$$

FORMULA SHEET

1. Arithmetic and geometric progressions

   a) n^{th} term of AP' $T_n = a + (n-1)d$

   b) Sum of AP: $S = \dfrac{n}{2}\left[2a + (n-1)d\right]$

   Or $S_n = \dfrac{n(a + T_n)}{2}$

   c) N^{th} term of GP: $T_n = AR^{n-1}$

   d) Sum of GP: $S_n = \dfrac{A(R^n - 1)}{R - 1}$ or $\dfrac{A(1 - R^n)}{(1 - R)}$

   e) Sum of GP to infinity: $S_\infty = \dfrac{A}{R - 1}$

Where a or A = first term
   d = Common difference
   R = Common ratio
   n = Number of terms

2. Compounding and Discounting

   a) simple interest $I = \dfrac{PTR}{100}$ or Pnr

   b) Amount of simple interest $S = P(1 + nr)$ or $P - Pnr$

   Where I = Simple interest
      R = Interest rate expressed as percentage
      r = interest rate expressed as proportion
      P = principal
      T = Time in years

   c) Compound interest: $S = P(1 + r)^n$

   d) Total interest: $I = P(1 + r)^n - P$

   Where S = Future value
      P = Principal
      r = Interest rate expressed or proportion
      n = Number of years
       I = Total interest

   e) Sum when interest rates change

$$S = P (1 + r_1)^x (1 + r_2)^{n-x}$$

Where S = future value
  P = principal
  r_1 = initial interest rate
  r_2 = next inter3est rate
  x = number of years in which r_1 applies
  n – x = Number of years in which r_2 applies.

f) Increasing the sum invested

$$S = P (1 + r)^n + \left[\frac{a (1 + r)^n - a}{r} \right]$$

Where P = Principal
  A = further amount invested
  n = The year to which the investment is valued
  r = Interest rate

g) Periodic rate = $\dfrac{\text{Annual Interest Rate}}{\text{Conversion Period}}$

h) Compound Amount: $A = P \left(1 + \dfrac{r}{m} \right) nm$

where P = Principal
  A = Compound amount
  m = Conversion period
  n = number of periods
  r = Nominal interest rate per annum

i) Effective Rate: $j = \left(1 + \dfrac{r}{m} \right)^{m} - 1$

Where j = Effective annual rate
  r = Nominal interest rate
  m = Number of conversion periods in a year

j) Present Value of a debt: $P = \dfrac{S}{1 + rn}$

Where P = present value of a debt
  S = maturity value of a debt
  n = number of years
  r = Simple interest

k) Simple Discount: I = Prn

Where I = Interest
  P = Principal
  r = Interest rate
  n = periods

l) Maturity value of simple discount

S = P (+ Prn or P (1 + rn)

m) Compound Discount: $P = \dfrac{A}{(1 + r)^n}$ or $P = A(1 + r)^{-n}$

Where P = Present value
A = Future value
r = Discount rate
n = Number of years

n) More Frequent Compound Discount

$$P = A \left[1 + \dfrac{r}{m} \right]^{-nm}$$

Where A = Future Value
n = Number of conversion Periods
R = Discount rate
m = Conversion frequency

o) Straight line Depreciation

$$D = \dfrac{C - R}{n}$$

Where D = Depreciation charge per annum
C = Cost of asset
R = Scrap value
n = Useful life in years

p) Common Depreciation

$$B = D (1 - r)^n$$

Where B = Book value
D = Cost of asset
r = Depreciation rate
n = Useful life in years

3. a) Internal Rate of Return (IRR)

$$IRR = A\% + \left(\dfrac{a}{a - b} (B - A)\% \right)$$

Where A = Lower discount rate
B = Higher discount rate
a = Positive NPV
b = Negative NPV

b) NPV = Present value of inflows – Present value of outflows.

4. a) Amount of an annuity

$$S = R \left(\dfrac{(1 + r)^n - 1}{r} \right)$$

b) Present value of an ordinary annuity

$$A = R \left[1 - \frac{(1 + r)^{-n}}{r} \right]$$

c) Present value of an annuity due

$$A = R + R \left[\frac{1 - (1 + r)^{-n}}{r} \right]$$

5. a) Coupon payment = Coupon rate X face value

b) Coupon rate = $\dfrac{\text{Coupon payment}}{\text{Par value}} \times 100$

c) Present value of pure discount bond

$$P = I \left[\frac{1 - (1 + r)^{-n}}{r} \right] + m (1 + r)^{-n}$$

Where I = Coupon payment
m = par value
n = Maturity period
r = Coupon rate

d) Present value of semi-annual coupon bond

$$P = I/2 \left[\frac{1 - (1 + r/2)^{-2n}}{r/2} \right] + M (1 + r/2)^{-2n}$$

Where P = Present value or purchase price
I = Coupon payment
M = Maturity value
r = Coupon rate
n = Maturity period

6. a) Expectation = PS or $\sum x \, P(x)$

Where P or P (x) = Probability
S or x = random variable

b) Present value of expectation:

$$PE = (1 + r)^{-n} PS \text{ or } PS (1 + r)^{-n}$$

Where PE = Present value
P = Probability
S = Future value
PS = Expectation
n = Number of periods
$(1 + r)^{-n}$ = Discount factor

c) Number of deaths within a year from age x to x + 1

$$d_x = L_x - L_x + 1$$

Where x = age

d) Cost of a pure endowment

$$_nE_x = (1 + r)^{-n} \frac{L_x + n}{L_x}$$

Where x = Age of a person now
n = Age when receiving the endowment
Lx + n = Number of people alive at age x + n
Lx = Number of people alive at age x
$_nE_x$ = Expectation present value
r = Interest rate (i.e. money worth)

e) For more frequent compounding expectation present value is:

$$A\left(1 + \frac{r}{M}\right)^{-mn} \left(\frac{L_x + n}{L_x}\right)$$

Where r = interest rate
m = frequency of compounding a year

f) Net single premium for ordinary whole life annuity

$$R \frac{N_x + 1}{D_x} = \text{Net single premium}$$

Where R = required annual payment
Nx – 1 = Age a person when first payment is due
Dx = Age of a person when annuity is taken

g) Net single premium for an ordinary temporary life annuity

$$\text{Net single premium} = \frac{R N_x + 1 - N_x - 1}{D_x}$$

Where Dx = Age of a person when annuity taken
Nx + 1 = Age of a person when first payment is made
Nx – 1 = Age of a person when last payment is made.

h) Net single premium for whole life insurance

$$\text{Net single premium} = I \frac{M_x}{D_x}$$

Where Mx = Age when policy is purchased
Dx = Age when amount is received
I = face value when the policy is purchased

i) Net single premium for a term insurance

Net single premium = I $\dfrac{Mx - Mx + n}{Dx}$

Where I = face value of policy
Mx = Age of a person when the policy is purchased
Mx + n = Age of a person when the policy matures
Dx = Age of a person when the policy is issued.

Number of Each Day of the year counting from January 1.

Day of month	Jan.	Feb.	Mar.	Apr.	May.	June.	July.	Aug.	Sept.	Oct.	Nov.	Dec.	Day of month
1	1	32	60	91	121	152	182	213	244	274	305	335	1
2	2	33	61	92	122	153	183	214	245	275	306	336	2
3	3	34	62	93	123	154	184	215	246	276	307	337	3
4	4	35	63	94	124	155	185	216	247	277	308	338	4
5	5	36	64	95	125	156	186	217	248	278	309	339	5
6	6	37	65	96	126	157	187	218	249	279	310	340	6
7	7	38	66	97	127	158	188	219	250	280	311	341	7
8	8	39	67	98	128	159	189	220	251	281	312	342	8
9	9	40	68	99	129	160	190	221	252	282	313	343	9
10	10	41	69	100	130	161	191	222	253	283	314	344	10
11	11	42	70	101	131	162	192	223	254	284	315	345	11
12	12	43	71	102	132	163	193	224	255	285	316	346	12
13	13	44	72	103	133	164	194	225	256	286	317	347	13
14	14	45	73	104	134	165	195	226	257	287	318	348	14
15	15	46	74	105	135	166	196	227	258	288	319	349	15
16	16	47	75	106	136	167	197	228	259	289	320	350	16
17	17	48	76	107	137	168	198	229	260	290	321	351	17
18	18	49	77	108	138	169	199	230	261	291	322	352	18
19	19	50	78	109	139	170	200	231	262	292	323	353	19
20	20	51	79	110	140	171	201	232	263	293	324	354	20
21	21	52	80	111	141	172	202	233	264	294	325	355	21
22	22	53	81	112	142	173	203	234	265	295	326	356	22
23	23	54	82	113	143	174	204	235	266	296	327	357	23
24	24	55	83	114	144	175	205	236	267	297	328	358	24
25	25	56	84	115	145	176	206	237	268	298	329	359	25
26	26	57	85	116	146	177	207	238	269	299	330	360	26
27	27	58	86	117	147	178	208	239	270	300	331	361	27
28	28	59	87	118	148	179	209	240	271	301	332	362	28
29	29	..	88	119	149	180	210	241	272	302	333	363	29
30	30	..	89	120	150	181	211	242	273	303	334	364	30
31	31	..	90	...	151	...	212	243	...	304	...	365	31

Commission 1941 Standard Ordinary Mortality Table

with Commutation Columns at $2\frac{1}{2}$%

Age x	Number Living lx	Number Dying dx	Dx	Nx	Mx	Age x
0	1,023,102	23,102				
1	1,000,000	5,770	975,609.76	30,351,127.80	235,338.3473	1
2	994,230	4,116	946,322.43	29,375,518.04	229,846.3782	2
3	990,114	3,347	919,419.28	28,429,195.61	226,024.2630	3
4	986,767	2,950	893,962.20	27,509,776.33	222,992.0462	4
5	983,817	2,715	869,550.88	26,615,814.13	220,384.6760	5
6	981,102	2,561	846,001.18	25,746,263.25	218,043.5400	6
7	978,541	2,417	823,212.53	24,900,262.07	215,889.0597	7
8	976,124	2,255	801,150.42	24,077,049.54	213,905.3152	8
9	973,869	2,065	779.804.53	23,275,899.12	212,099.6727	9
10	971,804	1,914	759,171.78	22,496,094.59	210,486.4980	10
11	969,890	1,852	739,196.60	21,736,922.86	209,027.7529	11
12	968,038	1,859	719,790.36	20,997,726.26	207,650.6874	12
13	966,179	1,913	700,885.94	20,277,935.90	206,302.1309	13
14	973,869	1,996	682,437.28	19,577,049.96	204,948.6727	14
15	962,270	2,069	664,414.29	18,894,612.68	210,486.4980	15
16	960,201	2,103	646,815.33	18,230,198.39	202,176.3495	16
17	958,098	2,156	629,657.27	17,583,383.06	200,794.2688	17
18	955,942	2,199	612,917.42	16,953,725.79	199,411.9146	18
19	953,743	2,260	596,592.68	16,340,808.37	198,036.3791	19
20	951,488	2,312	580,662.42	15,744,215.69	196,657.1668	20
21	949,171	2,382	565,123.40	15,163,553.27	195,280.6337	21
22	946,789	2,452	549,956.28	14,598,429.87	193,897.0141	22
23	944,337	2,531	535,153.17	14,048,473.59	192,507.4725	23
24	941,806	2,609	520,701.32	13,513,320.42	191,108.3791	24
25	939,197	2,705	506,594.02	12,992,619.10	189,700.8750	25
26	936,492	2,800	492,814.61	12,486,025.08	188,277.4101	26
27	933,692	2,904	479,357.22	11,993,210.47	186,839.8909	27
28	930,788	3,025	466,211.03	11,513,853.25	185,385.3418	28
29	927,763	3,154	453,361.83	11,047,642.22	183.907.1415	29
30	924,609	3,292	440,800.58	10,594,280.39	182,403.4951	30
31	921,317	3,347	428,518.18	10,153,479.81	180,872.3371	31
32	917,880	3,598	416,506.91	9,724,961.63	179,312.7277	32
33	914,282	3,767	404,755.37	9,308,454.72	177,719.8824	33
34	910,515	3,961	393,256.26	8,908,699.35	176,092.8950	34
35	906,554	4,161	381,995.63	8,510,443.06	174,423.8442	35
36	902,393	4,386	370,968.10	8,128,447.43	172,713.2832	36

37	898,007	4,625	360,161.02	7,757,459.33	170,954.2031	37
38	893,382	4,878	349,566.90	7,397,318.31	169,144,5103	38
39	888,504	5,162	339,178.75	7,047,751.41	167,282.3758	39
40	883,342	5,459	328,983.75	6,708,572.66	165,359.8889	40
41	887,883	6,785	318,976.11	6,379,589.05	163,376.3779	41
42	872,098	6,181	309,145.51	6,060,612.94	161,325.6832	42
43	865,967	6,503	299,485.04	5,751,467.43	159.205.3451	43
44	859,464	6,910	289,986.39	5,451,982.39	157,011.2084	44
45	852,554	7,340	280,638.95	5,161,996.00	154,736.6133	45
46	845,214	7,801	271,436.89	4,881,357.05	152,379.4034	46
47	837,413	8,299	262,372.33	4,609,920.16	149,935.2492	47
48	829,114	8,822	253,436.24	4,347,647.83	147,398.4842	48
49	820,292	9,392	244,624.00	4,094,111.59	144,767.6248	49

Commissioners 1941 Standard Ordinary Mortality Table
With commutation columns at 2½%

Age x	Number Living Lx	Number Dying dx	Dx	Nx	Mx	Age x
50	810,900	9,990	235,925.04	3,849,487.59	142,035.0956	50
51	800,910	10,628	227,335.17	3,613,562.55	139,199.4735	51
52	790,282	11,301	218,847.25	3,386,227.40	136,256.3361	52
53	778,981	12,020	210,456.33	3,167,380.15	133,203.1589	53
54	766,961	12,770	202,155.03	2,956.923.82	130,034.9360	54
55	754,171	13,560	193,940.61	2,754,768.79	126,751.1239	55
56	740,631	14,390	185,808.43	2,560828.18	123,349.2108	56
57	760,241	15,251	177,754.43	2,375,019.75	119,827.1207	57
58	710,990	16,147	169,777.17	2,197,265.32	116,185.3372	58
59	694,843	17,072	161,874.57	2,027,488.15	112,423.6404	59
60	677,771	18,022	154,046.23	1,865,613.58	108,543.4550	60
61	659,749	18,988	146,292.80	1,711,567.35	104,547.2551	61
62	640,761	19,979	138,616.97	1,565,274.55	100,439.5471	62
63	620,782	20,958	131,019.40	1,426,657.58	96,222.8711	63
64	599,824	21,942	123,508.39	1,295,638.18	91,907.4573	64
65	577,771	22,907	116,088.15	1,172,129.79	87.499.6261	65
66	554,975	23,842	108,767.29	1,056,041.64	83,010.1764	66
67	531,133	24,730	101,555.70	947,465.35	78,451.4482	67
68	506,403	25,553	94,465.545	845,718.651	73,838.2589	68
69	480,850	26,302	87,511.050	751,253.106	69,187.8068	69
70	454,548	26,955	80,706.625	663,742.056	64.517.7925	70

71	427,593	27,481	74,068.942	583,035.431	59,848.5665	71
72	400,112	27,872	67,618.148	508,966.489	55,204.3311	72
73	372,240	28,104	61,373.498	441,348.341	50,608.9030	73
74	344,136	28,154	55,355.921	379,974.843	46,088.2403	74
75	315,982	28,009	49,587.526	324,618.922	41,669.9911	75
76	287,973	27,651	44,089.787	275,031.396	37,381.7042	76
77	260,322	27,071	38,884.206	230,941.609	33,251.4840	77
78	233,251	26,262	33,990.850	192,057.403	29,306.5222	78
79	206,989	25,224	29,428.077	158,066.553	25,572.7964	79
80	181,765	23,966	80,706.625	663,742.56	64,517.7925	80
81	157,799	22,502	21,353.602	103,426.840	18,830.9965	81
82	135,297	20,857	17,862.047	82073.238	15,860.2597	82
83	114,440	19,062	14,739.984	64,211.191	13,173.8577	83
84	95,378	17,157	11,985.151	49.471.207	10,778.5365	84
85	78,221	15,185	9,589.4746	37,486.0561	8,675.1804	85
86	63,036	13,198	7,539.3905	27,896.5815	6,858.9858	86
87	49,838	11,245	5,815.4632	20,357.1910	5,318.9464	87
88	38,593	9,378	4,393.7546	14,514.7278	4,038.8010	88
89	29,215	7,638	3,244.7546	10,148.2505	2,997.2364	89
90	21,577	6,063	2,337.9929	6,903.4959	2,169.6149	90
91	15,514	4,681	1,640.0309	4,565.5030	1,528.6772	91
92	10,833	3,506	1,117.2571	2,925.4721	1,045.9042	92
93	7,327	2,540	737.2363	1,808.2150	693.1335	93
94	4,787	1,776	469.9158	1,070.9787	443.7944	94
95	3,011	1,193	288.3657	601.0629	273.7056	95
96	1,818	813	169.8646	142.8326	162.2378	96
97	1,005	551	91.6117	142.8326	88.1280	97
98	454	329	40.3755	51.2209	39.1261	98
99	125	125	10.8454	10.8454	10.5810	99

FEEDBACK

If you wish to send us any comments about this text, please complete the form below:

Name: ....

How have you used this Text?

- Home study (book only) ☐   - With "Correspondence" Package ☐

- On a course: College .... ☐   - Other ....

How did you obtain this Text?

- From Premier College ☐   - From your College ☐

- From Trafford publishing ☐   - Other ....

Your comments and suggestions would be appreciated on the following areas:

- Syllabus coverage

- Illustrative questions and solutions

- Errors (Please specify and refer to a page number)

- Presentation

- Other

Please return to:

Premier College of Banking and Finance

P.O. Box 34189 Lusaka